Musical Theatre

Musical Theatre

David Henson and Kenneth Pickering

 macmillan education  palgrave

First published 2017 by
PALGRAVE

Palgrave in the UK is an imprint of Macmillan Publishers Limited, registered in England, company number 785998, of 4 Crinan Street, London, N1 9XW.

Palgrave is a global imprint of the above companies and is represented throughout the world.

Palgrave® and Macmillan® are registered trademarks in the United States, the United Kingdom, Europe and other countries.

ISBN 978–1–137–60569–6 paperback

This book is printed on paper suitable for recycling and made from fully managed and sustained forest sources. Logging, pulping and manufacturing processes are expected to conform to the environmental regulations of the country of origin.

A catalogue record for this book is available from the British Library.

A catalog record for this book is available from the Library of Congress.

Contents

List of Illustrations

Acknowledgements

The authors wish to acknowledge and thank Marion Cox for her illustrations, Andrew Smith for his scoring of musical exercises, Dr Freya Vass-Rhee and students at the University of Kent for their help and inspiration; Sara Raybould, Director of London College of Music, staff and students at the University of West London (London College of Music) for trying out our ideas; composer and librettist Alex Loveless for his discussion; choreographers Chet Walker, Anthony Whiteman, Michael Thomas Voss, David Ashley, Emma Evans, George Kirkham and Barbara Hartwig for talking to us and allowing us to quote their opinions; Charlotte Emmett for her work on the MS; and our editor Nicola Cattini for her patience, help and encouragement.

Ways of Working

Introduction: Using This Book

This book is intended for anyone studying or teaching musical theatre at a college, university, conservatoire or private studio. It builds on the foundations we established in our previous *Workbook* (Palgrave, 2013) but can be used by anyone with some initial experience who wishes to engage in more in-depth study and develop the level of skill appropriate for a possible career in an aspect of musical theatre.

We hope that you will think of this book as a map to guide you through this stimulating and challenging world: a world that often seems to offer excitement and disappointment in equal measure. As you work your way through this book, we constantly invite you to make a thoughtful response to the topics we discuss: don't avoid this activity, for it is only by becoming a 'thinking performer' or 'reflective practitioner' that you will make any progress or achieve genuine originality in your work. Throughout this introductory section, we establish possible ways of working that provide a secure basis for your approach to what is, potentially, a demanding and fascinating subject.

You may find it best to work your way through this book stage by stage, but we would also advise you to look through its contents now and decide which chapters might be of most help: do not hesitate to use the material in any order you or your teachers find most suits your needs.

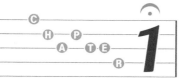

1 The World of Musical Theatre

You have probably realised that by deciding to become involved with musical theatre you have chosen to enter the world of the most popular form of live or recorded entertainment in recent history. But it is a rapidly and, sometimes, bewilderingly changing world. In this digital age you are able to access aspects of musical theatre in a way that would have been impossible and unthinkable only ten years ago. You can summon up performances from the distant past or from a few hours ago, and you can comment on what you see and hear with all the confidence of an arts critic. You can communicate your thoughts to a huge network of friends and the public, and even describe or reflect on what you are doing in a rehearsal or as a performance progresses.

Let us now think of some more examples of the changing face of performance in musical theatre. A recent development has been the relaying of 'live' performances from large theatres into cinemas: this may well indicate a trend for the future. It is possible, for instance, that most of the more lavish productions will be confined to a few very large theatres and that these will then be transmitted to cinema screens around the country. We may well move into an era of 'digital theatre', and in such situations the 'live' and new work might be confined to what we think of as 'fringe' or 'off Broadway' small-scale theatres. If you look at the theatre listings for any major city, you will see that this trend had already begun. But this is a different situation from seeing a musical on film, so what, precisely, is 'live performance'? At some 'transmitted' performances, members of the audience are invited to 'tweet' their comments, and these are displayed on the big screen during the interval.

Comment on some of the facts we have mentioned, and list other trends you have noticed in which the boundaries between 'live' and 'recorded' performance have become blurred.

In the opening sections of this book, we use a very well-known and popular piece of musical theatre, *The Sound of Music*, as an example. There are very good reasons for this choice. Perhaps the most significant is the fact that this work has established a unique position for itself in the history of the musical. Although *The Sound of Music* started life as a very successful stage show on Broadway in 1959, it is the movie version made in 1965 that has become best known. In his autobiography, *The Blue Touchpaper* (2015:3), the British playwright David Hare tells of a lady who watched the *Sound of Music* 365 times in a year, and you may have met someone with similar experiences. That film has spawned events like costumed 'singalongs' in cinemas, and if you are an enthusiast for musical theatre, it is highly likely that you have your own favourite songs that you could sing at will. *The Sound of Music* is probably the only musical to have prompted tour companies to organise holidays to the locations of the story. The popularity of the show was reinforced when the composer, Andrew Lloyd Webber, decided to mount a new production of it in London's West End and to select the performer who would play the lead role of Maria through a 'reality' TV show.

List in the box here the factors that would enhance the popularity of the show using this mode of casting.

A select number of the young performers who auditioned in this very public way were taken to a residential course where they were coached in singing, dancing and acting, and this demonstrated the emergence of what has become known as the 'triple-threat' performer: someone with high levels of skill in all three art forms.

Where do you think you stand in relation to this idea?

More recently, another new version of *The Sound of Music* was televised and broadcast in the United Kingdom at Christmas time, the traditional time for screenings of the old movie. This had very significant differences from the previous versions. Somewhat unusually, it was filmed in a theatre rather than on location, so the action and effects were limited by what could be achieved on a stage. The cast was almost entirely drawn from celebrity culture: performers known from TV. The lead role of Maria was played by Kara Tointon, who had become well known as a character in a favourite British soap opera, *EastEnders*, and then had enhanced her reputation by winning the reality show *Strictly Come Dancing* (or *Dancing with the Stars* as it is known elsewhere). Other roles were played by actors from popular TV costume dramas; the host of a frequently watched TV quiz game; and a familiar face from a reality cooking series. The influence of television, it seems, had become all pervasive.

If you have the opportunity, download and watch this version, and compare it with the original movie version. What do you notice about the performance style in the more recent version?

Many who watched the new TV version tweeted their opinions, and there was considerable anger that some of the songs had been placed at a different point in the action. On reflection it appears that the director, who included all the songs from both the original stage production and the subsequent movie, based the positioning of some of the songs not on their familiar place in the movie, but on the order in which they appeared in the stage show.

Discuss this issue and argue for the position of the songs in your 'ideal' production. Which two extra songs were written for the film version in 1965?

The lead performer in the TV version of *The Sound of Music* would probably describe herself as an actress who had discovered a real talent for dancing and who could sing adequately. She has certainly never claimed to be equally gifted in all three areas of performance. By contrast, the lead from the original movie version, Julie Andrews, would probably call herself a singer who could act a little and dance adequately. By comparing the two performers, we can trace the gradual emergence of the 'triple threat', but we might be forced to acknowledge that the creation of this 'ideal' being is neither possible nor even totally necessary: perhaps it is something to aim for in the knowledge that it is simply 'an ideal'? We discuss this issue frequently in the following pages.

What do you think and where do you see yourself in relation to the ideal of the 'triple threat'?

Technology has allowed us to create many 'performances' that might force us into thinking that we could never achieve such a level; but if we look more carefully and critically at some filmed versions, we can see how they sometimes disguise inadequacies. We need not feel intimidated!

For example, in the 1950s the famous Italian tenor Mario Lanza was considered too overweight to appear in the film of Sigmund Romberg's *The Student Prince*, and so his glorious voice was 'mimed' by the actor Edmund Purdom. Similarly, it was fairly obvious that some of the dancers in the first film of Rogers and Hammerstein's *Oklahoma!* were not singing and, like many pop stars who appeared in the early days of television, had not quite mastered the art of 'lip sync'. Even though sound and video technology have developed enormously since those days, we do now, in fact, rely even more on the versatility of the performer to convey a sense of truth. A far greater problem for you now, as a potential performer in musical theatre, is the temptation to model your work on what you can download or access via a recording, and this inevitably leads to mere imitation, lacking all originality. We reminded readers of our first Workbook of this problem, so from this point onwards, whatever you have done previously, remember that *you are an individual with a unique set of life experiences, tools and gifts* just waiting to be explored and developed.

What are the areas in your own performance that you feel you need to work on most?

Whatever your answers to the question we have just posed, you will discover that effective performance in musical theatre requires more than good singing, dancing and acting – or any combination of these. The ultimate key to performance lies in *understanding* the art form you are engaged with, and that theme runs through this book.

As a key aid to the process of understanding, we need to introduce and discuss the importance of maintaining a reflective journal as part of what, in essence, is a voyage of discovery.

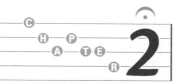

2 Creating a Reflective Journal

On the first page of this book, we introduced you to the concept of the 'reflective practitioner', and now we need to explore this idea further. It is important for you to understand that one of the most valuable tools you can employ in your studies in both practice and theory is to enrich your experience and deepen your understanding by appreciating the value of the 'reflective journal'. You will have written work diaries before and made records of personal and performance events in your life, but you may not have used a journal in the way we are now going to suggest.

We hope that this chapter goes some way to alleviating your fears regarding this 'written' work and enables you to realise the importance of such aspects of your study, even though we recognise that performing may be your ultimate goal. We want you to believe in the tasks we suggest as positive ways of achieving your ambitions.

Study the rest of this chapter very carefully so that you understand why you should take the time to record, reflect, analyse and ask questions about the many fascinating experiences you will encounter during your lifelong learning about musical theatre.

Many great artists in a wide variety of disciplines have employed critical writing as an invaluable source of ideas, questions, personal judgements and confidential thoughts. Amongst these was the famous artist and philosopher Leonardo Da Vinci (1452–1519):

> Thus I say to whom nature prompts to pursue his art, if you wish to have a sound knowledge of the forms of objects begin with the details of them, and do not go to the next step till you have the first well fixed in memory and practice. And if you do otherwise you will throw away your time, or certainly greatly prolong your studies. And remember to acquire diligence rather than rigidity... Any master who should venture to boast that he could remember all the forms and effects of nature would certainly appear to me to be graced with extreme ignorance, inasmuch as these effects are infinite and our memory is not extensive enough to retain them.
>
> (Da Vinci, p. xi)

The art of reflection might appear at first mention to be a relaxed, calm and passive occupation – it is not! Involvement in musical theatre activities requires active thought and, more importantly, the ability to constantly ask questions without always expecting to find answers. Writing about what you have done and your opinions about the work are definitely not the point of the exercise. We are not encouraging you to write a diary of events, we want you to be able to discover factors regarding the creative process that have not yet been considered in your work. As an element of your performance progress, your teachers might ask you to take risks and experiment with ideas. You may well find this difficult because you are worried about being judged or assessed. Our aim is to provide you with the confidence to work free of these anxieties.

Consider the following questions: how do we know what we know about a specific musical?

Why are we confident in our explanation?

No matter what answers you have written to these two questions, the answer will have relevance and integrity for you as a thinker and performer. You might have found, for instance, that your answers actually rely on your position and experience in society. If possible, compare your answers with those of other students to see what they think. Having discussed these questions and your answers, you will observe that people have many ways of considering what we might have thought was obvious, and so we should always be prepared to challenge and reconsider ideas. After all, the world was thought to be flat until someone had the audacity to challenge the presumed 'obvious' fact. The essence of this is that your experiences in performance do not, in themselves, make you a wise performer.

So you need to adopt a method of working that will help to develop both your mental and performance skills. As we have seen, it is the questions that are important, so do not become overanxious to find quick answers. When ideas occur, however randomly, always make a note of them, discuss them with your teachers and find out why you think they might be meaningful for you. They may well open up a new way of thinking and give you a different perspective on the work in progress. The *light-bulb* moment is always very rewarding.

Moments of reflective thinking have a narrative sequence which should be recognised when planning an entry in your reflective journal. You might, for example, have a sudden thought in a dance session about breath and its inspiration for a specific movement and how it empowered you to do something in class. This might have surprised you so much that you wrote the original thought down in a moment of reflection. Subsequently, you realised how this idea fascinated you, so you noted down personal reactions over a period of time.

Consider some of the following points, with specific examples:

1. What were your original responses to a particular idea?
2. Have they now changed and given you new insights into the work?
3. Has the idea set up a series of questions?
4. Identify the reaction of others to your ideas.

By acknowledging these stages of thinking, there will be a clear development in your understanding of the original idea, and you will also learn more about your own thinking process. Be brave and consider this as an important part of your practice. In this way your approach will become more insightful and confident, and you will become more aware of your creative self. You might ask, 'What is creativity, and why is it important to us as performers?' There have been numerous answers to this question, and many definitions, but we would argue that it is the lifeblood of our performance, and we need to recognise that, in order to be creative, we must be engaged and focused with every aspect of our work both emotionally and intellectually.

> A new world calls across the ocean
> A new world calls across the sky
> A new world whispers in the shadows
> Time to fly, time to fly…
>
> (Jason Robert Brown, *Songs for a New World*, 1995)

Yes, it is a new world and indeed a *'time to fly'*, so start to consider your performance career with renewed energy and vitality.

Perhaps the essential ingredient of work in musical theatre is the recognition of how we see ourselves as part of it and what we believe we can achieve. Look at the following questions, and use them as a starting point for your journal. This might take some time, but if you are going to progress effectively, you need to be aware of your strengths and weaknesses as soon as possible.

With some care and attention, write a personal 'skills audit' of all your achievements in the field of performance so far. Think carefully, and be brave in your decisions. If you feel you are very good at something, then say so. Be explicit by describing the skills you actually possess in all areas of performance.

List the subjects you are currently studying or are going to study. Identify which skills have been useful to each area of performance, and explain why.

There are many other factors to consider when studying performance, but you will find as you reflect on your practice that many of the problems you encounter will be overcome if you are *better prepared*. For this reason, Part Three of this book is largely devoted to this important topic, and you may wish to turn to it now to ascertain what is involved in the most effective means of preparation.

Time is precious for students, and many regret the time wasted during their first year of study. Here are some personal hints to help you make your future studies more effective and meaningful:

1. Always ensure that you give sufficient time to preparing for the next session in each subject.
2. Avoid 'playing' at being a performer rather than realising the effort that is needed to achieve a high level of skill.
3. Use your peers to help you develop skills outside of the taught sessions.
4. Always look beyond the lesson, to the future, and aim to read as much as possible.
5. Keep thinking about your own practice, and challenge your ideas and where they come from.

Remember that the reflective journal is a document where you *can* express your own ideas and challenge them without fear. Enjoy this position as a student and critical thinker, and you will soon see the benefits when working with others in the studio or rehearsal space.

It is not always easy to prepare for the moment when you are required to challenge your own approach and hear other opinions regarding your work. At this point you have to make decisions about your role and position as part of the process and accept the rules that go with this activity. Receiving feedback from teachers and directors can sometimes be a difficult experience. The object of the exercise, of course, is for you to remain focused and engaged while understanding that all the information given you is for your future development as a performer. Sometimes you will be asked to break old habits in order to progress. Being asked to travel into the unknown is demanding, but it enables you to experience a greater sense of creativity. Arriving at new thinking is frequently a result of receiving constructive criticism or of entering into a dialogue.

Clearly, reflection is very personal and often based upon an individual's education and perceived social standing. But we need to be honest about the traits we bring to our decision-making, and we suggest that you explore your approaches using the following exercise.

Identify *five* personality traits listed below that might describe you when defending or proposing an idea.

Analytical
Argumentative
Arrogant
Confident
Constructive
Creative
Critical
Emotional
Irrational
Irritable
Objective
Optimistic
Rational
Reliable
Subjective

Choose one of the five personality descriptors, and discuss how this has affected some of your work in an area of learning, rehearsal or performance.

If you had approached the same problem from a different standpoint, how do you think it might have been solved? How do you feel about all this?

It is important to be aware of your personality and to be able to look at problems through new eyes in order to gain objective and perhaps more truthful points of reflection. This will all take time, but it is worth applying to all aspects of your work – written or practical.

Enquiry is a lifelong habit, and by considering our lives from different perspectives, we can recognise the power of self. This enables us to solve problems at all levels of our study and become the performer that everyone wants to work with.

Try to remain fascinated, not intimidated, by the unknown. When you can't find a solution to a problem, leave it alone for a while, and come back to it later: then suddenly it may become clear. 'Time', as the composer Hector Berlioz once said, 'is a great teacher,' and will often enable you to formulate responses to tricky questions. The art of daydreaming is also a useful tool for the creative thinker and performer. Allow such moments to occur during your leisure time, and let your creative spirit develop.

There will be many stylistic issues for you to consider when writing your reflective journal. The overuse of the personal pronoun 'I' is often best avoided in order to give your writing a more balanced and philosophical detachment. Express your ideas as a public forum. Do not over-plan your writing or constantly seek to justify your actions. Allow your writing to be an exploration of your own contradictions. Once an idea is on the page, try to work out why it is there.

Your writing will be similar to the way you look at yourself in a recent passport picture. You are never satisfied: you want to destroy it or take another one. You see yourself differently from the way others see you. Nothing will change until you start accepting this. Write about your personal feelings with the awareness that someone needs to understand what you have written.

There is one final note of warning with regard to your personal thinking. We are now in an era of communication technology, and you may be encouraged to maintain a journal through video diaries or blogs. Be aware of your life as a blogger, tweeter, emailer, Facebook account member, texter, website owner or online personality. Remember that everything communicated through electronic means may be recorded and stand to bite you at any time in the future. Take care. With this in mind it is sometimes safer to communicate your ideas to yourself in a confidential written reflective journal, with the knowledge that it will only be viewed by agreed individuals.

Now that we have looked at some of the essential ingredients of your journal, you should realise that it is a very individual and personal item that can become a companion and support, and can be vital to your future success as both artist and thinker.

Learning achieved through practice is an important aspect of your studies. Reflection is an essential part of that process, as it constitutes the ability to develop an understanding of what you aim to achieve. Individual work in any area of performance technique will always involve imagination, focus and preparation. But for each subject, there also may be different demands. A useful way of working is to identify three areas in any one subject and measure your progress in these until you are satisfied with your level of improvement. Then, replace the improved task with another so that you are continually making yourself aware of what you have achieved and have yet to achieve.

The following exemplar record sheet is designed to assist you in your personal and mental development and could form part of your reflective journal.

PERSONAL PROFILE

SUBJECT DISCIPLINE: **DATE:**

Mental and physical state	*ASSESSMENT LEVEL* *1 = Lots of work needed; 10 = Very pleased with progress*									
	1	2	3	4	5	6	7	8	9	10
Motivation										
Anxiety										
Relaxation										
Concentration/focus										
Use of imagery										
Determination										
Confidence										
Physical well-being										
Distractions										
Enjoyment										

Mental and Physical State	**Assessment Level (date)**	**Review of Assessment Level (date)**

Personal notes on three aspects of your work and approach

How do you intend to improve on your personal scores?

What personal tasks and goals were set?

PROBLEMS IDENTIFIED:

SOLUTIONS:

2 Understanding Musical Theatre

Using Part Two

If you are studying musical theatre, is it almost certain that you have spent and will increasingly spend many hours preparing for and performing in extracts or entire stage works that integrate the arts of music, dance and drama. In other words, you are engaged with the distinctive genre that has come to be known as 'the musical'. In Part One of this book, we outlined some of the current characteristics of this form of theatre and offered some guidance on how to equip yourself to participate effectively in your studies. Now, however, we need to introduce you to modes of analysis and investigation that will enrich your knowledge and deepen your understanding of the musical. Sometimes students are so caught up in learning songs or scenes that they overlook the importance of extending their horizons to encompass every aspect of a work. Their approach remains superficial, and they cannot place whatever they are learning to perform in a wider context. Such students are unable to discuss, write about or reflect upon their experience at an appropriate level.

All too often the world of education encourages situations in which students are swamped with information emanating from the preconceived ideas of authors. The aim of this book is unashamedly to enable you, the reader, to develop your own judgements and opinions. We hope that both knowledge and wisdom will be at the centre of your observations.

There are many examples of books containing adequate analyses of the musical in all its shapes and forms (see Bibliography). The intention of this section is to enhance your own ideas and give you structured ways of thinking that can form part of your unique approach to the works you encounter. Investigating a specific musical and its score requires a detailed research programme and often the assistance of a teacher to guide you in your thoughts. At this point, we are enabling you to discover facts for yourself and boost your confidence in exploring and interrogating the art form in the depth that it deserves.

Once again we shall begin by using *The Sound of Music* as an example.

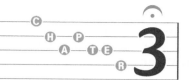

The Making of a Musical

Shortly before this book was written an extraordinary event in the world of musical theatre took place in Salzburg, Austria: a theatre in the city mounted a production of the most popular film-musical of all time, *The Sound of Music* by Rodgers and Hammerstein. What was remarkable about this occurrence was that, although *The Sound of Music* describes events in and around Salzburg and, as we have mentioned earlier, busloads of tourists have flocked to the area to see the real locations shown on stage and film, there had never before been a local production of this musical written almost seventy years ago.

You may care to speculate at this point as to why this should be. Was it, perhaps, that the citizens of Salzburg were uncomfortable about the welcome given to Hitler when he occupied the city with his Nazis in the early days of the Second World War? Or was it that the romantic story of a girl, immortalised by the singing of Julie Andrews, who left a convent to become governess to the children of the navy Captain von Trapp, teaches the children to sing, marries the Captain and takes part in a daring escape over the mountains into Switzerland is too remote from the actual truth?

A TV documentary about the recent production showed many people interviewed in the streets of Salzburg being totally ignorant of or indifferent to the songs and characters from *The Sound of Music.* What we now know is that Maria von Trapp, on whose autobiography the show is apparently based, was anything but the sweet and slightly air-headed former Nun who was told by her Mother Superior to 'Climb Every Mountain'. She, rather than the Captain, was controlling and authoritarian, she certainly did not teach the children to sing: that task was undertaken by a talented priest who eventually accompanied the family when they re-located to the USA and, perhaps most disappointing of all, the family did not escape over the mountains in apparent fulfilment of the Mother Superior's wish, but by train to Italy!

So we reluctantly come to the conclusion that the wonderful singing lesson: 'Doe, a deer, a female deer, Ray, a drop of golden sun' and so on, is pure fantasy; as is much else in this enormously popular musical. Why, then, is *The Sound of Music* so successful and what can we learn about the way a musical is created by considering this example?

To the first question we might initially answer, 'the tunes are totally memorable' because Richard Rodgers captures all the moods, drama and tensions of the story, or we might suggest that Oscar Hammerstein II, one of the greatest librettists of all time, creates words that celebrate music, nature and love, (as he does in several other works) with wit, charm and easily remembered rhythms and rhyme schemes.

We might also add that this musical has certain appealing ingredients: love, children, excitement, humour and spectacular scenery. But every one of the factors we have mentioned is the result of choices and decisions made at an early stage by the writers. Recognising the nature of these decisions will enable us to perform this, or any other work, with insight, sensitivity and awareness. We can learn about the process of making artistic decisions by thinking more about this musical.

Later in this chapter we shall consider some of the various forms that a musical might take and that form will usually depend on the basic ideas that set the writers on their creative journey. The initial 'creative team' of dramatists may well include a choreographer and they may be joined at a later stage by a producer, designer and director.

The initial idea

Books and plays

The initial stimulus for *The Sound of Music* was a story contained in a book. There are many familiar examples of books and plays as starting points for musicals: H.G.Wells's *Kipps,* became the musical *Half a Sixpence*, Dickens's *Oliver Twist* and *The Pickwick Papers* became *Oliver* and *Pickwick,* Victor Hugo's *Les Miserables* was turned into a musical of the same name; Shakespeare's *Romeo and Juliet*, *The Taming of the Shrew* and *Othello* were transformed into *West Side Story, Kiss me Kate* and *Catch my Soul* respectively and Lynn Rigg's play *Green Grow the Lilacs* inspired *Oklahoma!* The extent to which these musicals adhered to their original source varied considerably but, as with *The Sound of Music* it is true to say that they were new works with their own distinctive form and were often fairly loosely based on the source. Even if some of the original dialogue from the book or play is included in the musical or used as the basis for song lyrics, a considerable amount of reshaping and additional writing is required to create a satisfactory new stage work.

Themes and concepts

Many successful musicals are built around entirely original story lines and will often explore a particular aspect of life or a cultural phenomenon. Some will examine the life of the Theatre itself with all its disappointments and triumphs; others may be based around dance crazes or fashions or celebrate the life of a particular entertainer. Other musicals may take an historical event or figure and present a new perspective on the subject, sometimes satirical and sometimes fiercely critical.

RESEARCH ACTIVITY
List examples of works that fulfil some of the descriptions above.

The 'Jukebox musical'

You will probably have noticed that in the latter part of the 20th and now in the 21st century much of the musical theatre source material has been inspired either by the works of notable singers such as Elvis Presley, Cliff Richard or Buddy Holly or by vocal groups such as ABBA with *Mamma Mia!* or Queen with *We Will Rock You*. Such shows are often a response to immediate audience appeal and a wish to celebrate the culture of a particular time and generation. Audiences will gain enjoyment from their familiarity with the musical score. There are interesting forces at work here: the necessity for a musical to be a commercial as well as an artistic success means that the choice of subject material is often a decisive factor in the making of the work. Few theatrical managements would spend three years creating a musical if audiences were not going to want to hear it or if it is only going to last until previews and never get to opening night! Nevertheless, failures of this kind are remarkably frequent.

RESEARCH ACTIVITY
List examples of works that are based on the work of popular singers, groups and bands.

Real-life stories

Often, an ideal choice for the subject of a musical will be the story of an individual or group who have made an impact upon the lives of others for good or for more dubious reasons. Obvious examples would be *Evita* (based on the life of Eva Peron) by Andrew Lloyd Webber and Tim Rice, *Side Show,* a musical centred on the life of the Hilton Sisters by Henry Krieger and Bill Russell and two musicals about Marilyn Monroe. *The King and I,* and *The Sound of Music* by Rodgers and Hammerstein or *Barnum* by Mark Drumble, Michael Stewart and Cy Coleman are all examples of musicals where aspects of or incidents from a real-life story are involved.

However, because the creation of a musical is an artistic venture and there are many other forces at play, the accuracy of the events and the truth of the situations may be rewritten in order to enable the musical to have a structure that is plausible for an audience seeking an evening's entertainment. We have already seen that the Maria of *The Sound of Music* is not the Maria of the real-life situation but this is an example of where historical truth is replaced by artistic truth as it is in the so-called 'History Plays' of Shakespeare

RESEARCH ACTIVITY

Consider people from the worl of show business who you think have a worthwhile life-story to transform into a musical. Suggest why and how their life would suit the form of a musical. Be inventive and have some fun.

Discover as many musicals as you can that fit in this category and any common factors affecting their success or failure.

Decisions to be made in the creation of a musical

Forces

When a creative team or individual sets out to construct a musical and decides what its story-line or topic might be they must then obtain a clear idea of the forces for which they are writing. Are they, for example, writing for a large cast with a full orchestra and a spacious stage or, conversely, are they writing for a small number of performers with, perhaps, a single keyboard and drums accompaniment in a more intimate theatre? With the spiralling costs of production and the growing popularity of musicals there have recently been many more examples of the latter. But production managements also continue to invest heavily in huge productions that rely on sophisticated technology, spectacular choreography and 'star' billings. Of course, once a musical is in a completed form it may later be adapted for slightly different forces but its nature will largely be determined by its original conception.

RESEARCH ACTIVITY
What other considerations concerning resources do you think may shape a musical?

Form

The form of a musical will be determined by the nature of the story or theme and how this is related to an audience using the available resources. If the work is to be the re-telling of a complex story, possibly set in some other historical period, it may well have a number of leading characters and a chorus who make up a 'crowd' commenting on the action. On the other hand, if the work is a series of scenes and songs based on a theme or a story in which all the 'characters' are equally involved, it is likely that it will demand a cast who work as an ensemble and have equal skills in acting, singing and dancing. They might take turns at being the main character- focus for a while and then blend back into the ensemble as someone else takes 'centre stage'. Both Stephen Sondheim and Michael Bennett showed themselves to be particularly skilful in writing such 'company' musicals.

Dancing, singing and choreography

In what we might loosely term 'Western' cultural traditions it has not been normal to combine singing with dancing but in African, South American and various Eastern traditions this is certainly not the case. It is, for example, unthinkable that a group of African or Afro-Caribbean singers would not dance as they sing. In the early years of development of musical theatre in nineteenth-century Paris, London or Vienna, there was plenty of singing and of dancing but they tended to be separate entities. When, however, many of these traditions blended with the African-American, Jewish and Irish musical worlds in the United States we see the emergence in the early years of the twentieth century of what we now recognise as 'choreography' in the flowering 'musical theatre'. When, in the musical comedy *Oklahoma!* (1944) the choreographer Agnes de Milne, succeeded in making dance an integral part of the action and an almost equal partner with singing and acting, the role of dance was transformed for ever. How, when and why you dance in a musical will be one of the key questions to explore in the course of your studies.

The idea of a 'chorus'

The idea of a chorus is as old as Theatre itself and is often thought of as a group of singers, speakers and dancers who comment on the action of the main characters. More recently, especially in forms of musical theatre, the chorus has sometimes been like a choir standing behind the main action or a group of singer/dancers who introduce a show. This certainly remains the case in pantomimes, where production companies will often recruit their 'chorus' from local dance schools.

However, modern theatre practice has tended to move away from the chorus as a mainly static or decorative feature and has established the idea that chorus members are characters within their own rights. Huge physical, creative and vocal demands are now made on members of the chorus and they are expected to be fully involved in the emotional and physical situations in which they appear. This, in turn, has inspired writers to make much more creative use of the chorus and, in some cases, to make the entire chorus into the central character.

Not only is it vital for you to understand the role of the chorus in any production in which you are taking part but it is also essential that you realise that being cast as a member of the chorus is as challenging and rewarding as being cast as a leading individual character.

RESEARCH ACTIVITY
Identify examples of the various uses and functions of the chorus that we have discussed.

Shape of the action

Once a theme or story has fixed itself in the minds of the maker of musicals the next process involves decisions about the shape of the work to be created. Will it for example, resemble a substantial Three Act play with clearly defined climaxes for each Act and an interval in the middle? Or will it be a continuous stream of action without a break? How many characters will be on stage at any time and will they speak or sing? Perhaps, more importantly for us, if they sing or dance WHY do they do that and how do they move from speaking into singing and/or dancing without seeming ridiculous?

A strong narrative line will be created by the writer of the 'book' of the show but the composer *and choreographer* will have a vital role in enhancing that narrative. At some point, however, both the director and performer will contribute to giving the work a stage life. In the case of an entirely new musical this may involve experimenting with the material to enable the writers to make revisions and changes but with an established work the director and performer still make an essential contribution to the process of creating a new life for the work.

An approach to the analysis of a musical: talking with writers

At a recent composers' workshop, William Finn suggested that it is the ability to '...use tools rather than rules' that is vital when writing musicals. That ability is, of course, precisely what we want to achieve at this stage in your studies.

Following the dialogue below with the dramatist/composer Alex Loveless, you should begin to understand those important factors that constitute a musical and be able to look for these when you are engaged in your own personal analysis of a musical score and libretto.

As we entered the world of the creative artist who has conceived a musical based on Thomas Hardy's *Tess of the d'Urbervilles* we wanted to discover his approach, motivation and intention in writing this piece. Obviously, it would assist your understanding were you to be able to refer to the original novel:

DH   Why did you choose to write a musical based on Thomas Hardy's *Tess of the d'Urbervilles?*

AL   Well to be honest, owing to the nature of the art form, there have to be two main reasons for writing – artistic and commercial. We all have to make a living! The artistic element is the persuasive argument to create, and so the inspiration for the musical must have a powerful storyline with potential for atmospheric locations that will drive the writer to complete the project. There need to be opportunities for the characters to exist within a believable situation and yet have the potential to speak, sing and dance. A timeless quality and a sense of the spiritual were also exciting to consider as part of the texture of the musical. I was very interested in writing a score influenced by folk music and its attendant timeless qualities – indeed it is folk music's simplicity and immediacy that make it such a potent tool. There is a great deal of cross-over between the musical vocabulary of folk music and pop music (modally, harmonically, rhythmically) which gives it an air of familiarity to the modern listener. Perhaps this could also impact upon the ease of staging so that the acoustic quality of the folk melodies can be dealt with in a variety of small or large venues. Of course the powerful protagonist (main character) of Tess was a real pull for me as a writer and composer. In terms of the show's commercial potential it is useful to have a title that an audience will know and so be attracted to immediately. Tess is a highly evocative figure, especially for women in the 21st century, and as a result has the potential to be a star vehicle for a well-known performer. The novel is out of copyright – always a bonus when considering the commercial implications of a musical.

DH   The novel is clearly structured to identify stages of development in the story of Tess. How did you deal with the various sections in this novel?

AL   I actually declined to be controlled by the seven stages of the novel's structure and aimed for a more continuous dramatic through-line. It is important for a musical to have pace and action and by not being bound by the existing structure I felt I was able to generate greater dramatic intensity. I amalgamated characters to ensure a manageable cast size and avoid audience confusion. I was also aware of the cost of casting a production. I felt it necessary to streamline some of the more obscure contemporaneous philosophical arguments contained within the novel relating to different strands of religious belief and some layers of character motivations as they would have taken too long to explain and become dramatically unsatisfying. In my version the character of Angel doubts all religious belief rather than one particular creed. When Angel leaves Tess after discovering the truth about Alec it has to be very clear why he does this (i.e. the audience can't be asked to pay attention while you list twenty possible reasons) and, for the sake of dramatic intensity and time, this needs to be more of an emotional knee-jerk reaction than a considered response. The use of a chorus, as in Greek tragedy, was also an essential concept in this musical to establish seasons, time and place.

DH   How did your ideas develop into the structure of a musical and a response to the probable demands of an audience's expectations?

AL   I did exactly what I would want a performer to do when looking at the musical for the first time. I first read through the novel quite quickly. I then returned to it again and allowed myself to reflect upon the detail of the writing and the images that captured my imagination. I started to find times when the inner reflection of the character could be expressed in song. I then listened to the voice of each character for its musicality in terms of both speech patterns and range. Variety and conflict should be present at every opportunity whether it is in text, vocal line or plot.

DH   The novel recognises the importance of the seasons and the passing of time; (present, recent and distant past) how did this work for you when writing the libretto and score?

AL   The chorus enables not only the passing of time and seasons to be expressed with clarity and pace but also emphasises the symbolism of the seasons e.g. Spring for birth and late Summer for the sowing of the seed. Such metaphors as 'what we sow, we reap' are fulfilled by the body of players who constitute the chorus. This is a device to move from season to season rapidly and enable the audience to follow the action.

DH   The title of novel and musical indicates that Tess is central to the structure of the musical? How did your writing reflect this? Did the music reflect these changes?

AL   Tess is the main character in this musical. All other characters exist only as they relate to her wants and desires. We are not interested in either Angel or Alec when they are off stage but when they engage with Tess we are able to observe in some detail her emotional journey and development and sense of her position, status and predicament within the overall structure. Tess has the only two solo ballads in the musical with all other characters having to share musical material - so this isolation of the main character is further enhanced and enforced by the musical structure. The different harmonic textures estab-lished within the sung material for Tess enable us to identify significant changes within her character and persona as the musical develops. We move from the folk element at the beginning of the musical to a semi operatic quality by the end of the work when she is presented as the mistress of Alec.

DH   Did you ever consider the idea of transporting this character into a more contemporary context?

AL   Personally I feel, the environment and period Tess inhabits are central to the plot and mirror many of Tess's internal struggles through pathetic fallacy (the ache of modernity as a centuries-old way-of-life is swept away and new value systems are imposed). Sometimes the setting of a novel does seem arbi-trary and then one feels less compunction about removing the action to a dif-ferent setting / period or contemporising it.

DH   Let's talk about your treatment of what may now seem to be archaic lan-guage – such words as 'verily'; how did you treat this? What was important to you?

AL   Retaining a sense of the rich Wessex dialect was essential. But some pas-sages were so 'thick' that they needed simplification. You can't re-read a line that an actor delivers on stage! The song lyrics often become internal mono-logue or the character's truth and as such demand a slightly different treat-ment. The thoughts are tighter as we don't think in full sentences and are not hide-bound by social mores when having a conversation with ourselves. It was of course necessary to avoid glaring anachronisms or inappropriate vocabulary but, just as one would not attempt to sing with a thick West County accent, nor does one need to faithfully replicate a Wessex dialect in a song lyric – a nod in the right direction here and there is quite enough.

Points for reflection and discussion arising from the interview

In addition to the **three main characters** in *Tess of the d'Urbervilles* providing conflict and resolution within the action, we also have **supporting minor characters** to add context and purpose to specific scenes and a **chorus of men and women** commenting on the action and representing the passage of time. Thus, we have a perfect demonstration of the six elements of **tragedy** as expressed by Aristotle in his famous work *Poetics* dated 330 BC [approx.] Do not be alarmed by the word 'tragedy' because Aristotle's work has become the basis for much of the structure used in Western drama, even in the 21st century. The six elements and their relevance to *Tess* are:

1. Plot   This is formed from the events in the text: one incident follows another in a sequential progression.

2. Character   Often the main character is of little significance until their life is affected by those around them.

3. Ideas   The thoughts of the characters are revealed to the audience and their plans and decisions are communicated as the scene progresses.

4. Dialogue   This is the means by which all the characters communicate with each other and through which the audience is able to follow the individual thoughts, reasons and actions of each character.

5. Melody   Often solo songs enable individual thoughts to be expressed and the chorus is able to comment upon the action or on the universal ideas embedded in the text and action.

6. Spectacle   This is the visual amplification of the situation so that the audience is carried along not only by the language but by the visual aspects of the story. In a musical this visual spectacle is often paramount to its success with choreography, moving set and scenery sometimes overshadowing the actual drama of the situation. Think, for example of *Phantom of the Opera* and the spectacular collapse of the chandelier at end of Act One and the candlelit boat journey through the underworld of the Paris Opera House.

With points raised in our interview in mind now look closely at a musical you are studying and consider the following questions and engage with the exercises:

- Identify plot points contained in the musical. How are these divided up in terms of dialogue / song?
- How do the songs interact with the libretto? Do the songs show and explore feelings, continue a personal story/situation, tell the audience something they didn't know before or reveal a secret?
- Having worked out the plot are you ready to tell the story to an audience? What excites and intrigues you about this story?
- Tell the story from the perspective of one character and explore any conflicts that might occur from this vantage point.
- Now tell the story as an observer/ reporter/ member of the ensemble.
- What has happened off stage and how do you know about it? What clues are there in the text?
- Look at the moments when each character is required to sing. What is the justification for this?

Now let us put some of these observations to the test by considering a musical theatre scene of your own choosing.

Considering the **text** first:

- Did you relate to the story being told on a personal level?
- Do you think the story inspires the audience and enables them to be fully engaged with the characters and their believable situations?
- Is the plot structure easy to follow?
- Do the events follow naturally?
- Does the writing provide emotional conflict or tension?
- Is there an opportunity for spectacle?
- Are the words able to express the emotions and conflicts rather than just the story line?
- What do the characters say about each other?
- Are we allowed to discover facts rather than being told them?
- Does the text intrigue and fascinate you?

Now the **musical score**

- Do you find the songs pleasing to the ear?
- Are there interesting contrasts within each song – dynamic changes – soft to loud; rhythmic changes – simple beats to syncopated rhythms etc.?
- Do the vocal ranges imitate each other or is there a contrast in the vocal intensity of the solo songs?
- If orchestrated, what do you notice about the texture of the orchestration: varied, similar, different instrumentation?
- Can you find the simple structure of each musical number?
- Do the songs fit the action and the emotional needs of the characters?

Finally, the **lyrics**

- Do the songs emerge easily from both action and text?
- Does the style of the songs and the vocal range suit the individual characters?
- What vocal qualities may be used to express the meaning of the lyrics?
- Does the quality of the lyrical language match that of the spoken dialogue?

We hope that we have now established a way of working and of approaching the musical theatre repertoire that will remain with you for the rest of your creative life. The experience of investigating and asking questions about a scene, combined with all the exercises and research activities that we have provided throughout this book, should enable you to develop into a true artist bringing a profound sense of integrity to all that you do. Indeed, we aim to enable you to make any musical you are working on 'your own' and this is the focus of our next, short chapter.

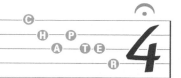

Making the Musical Your Own

However much you may learn about the structure, history or writing of a musical, this knowledge will remain virtually useless unless you are able to apply it to any performance in which you are involved. Once you have been cast in a piece of musical theatre, you must move on to take ownership of the material from the moment that you first read the script and score or watch and/or listen to a recording. In this initial stage you need to identify what is important for you as a performer in the show and achieve a very clear understanding of the **demands it will make** on you. You also need to refine your ideas of precisely how your role will contribute to the whole and what an audience will 'read' from every aspect of the performance.

Every time you participate in a musical that has been written and performed previously, you are engaged in giving it what the director Jonathan Miller described as 'an afterlife'. In other words, the show must be born again, with the production team and performers as midwives in this process. This means that you must approach the material with entirely fresh attitudes, not depending on what you may have seen or heard before. Difficult decisions must be made: will you, for example, use the original choreography, or will you model your performance on that of an original star of the show? If you follow this approach, do you recognise the danger of simply engaging in a kind of archaeology: digging up the past rather than creating something new and meaningful for today's world? You may, of course, have little control over some of these decisions because they will be made by the director, music director, choreographer and designer, *but* you must understand the decisions and recognise how they impact on what you are required to do.

In order to achieve this level of preparedness before you even begin to participate in learning words, moves and music, or in rehearsals, you will, once again, need to ask many questions. In order to help you with this process, we pose a single important question about your approach to the whole 'work' (as we shall now call the chosen musical) and then consider the elements of music, drama and dance.

The work

The fundamental question to consider is whether the work is a fixed and final entity that must be performed in the way suggested by the script and score or by the way in which it was first directed, performed or recorded; *or* can that original work be used as a basis for new interpretation and variations introduced by a contemporary production team?

Think back now to the information we supplied about the recent TV production of *The Sound of Music*. The song 'Climb Every Mountain', sung by the Mother Superior of the Convent, has usually been sung by an operatic performer as a very big number accompanied by chorus and choreography. Presented like this the song is inspirational and cosmic in its philosophical content. But in the TV production, it was presented almost as a conversational and intimate piece of advice. Was this *wrong* or just a matter of interpretation for our far less formal age? Did this provoke a sense of frustration or surprise in you, or did it seem like a refreshing change? Did this approach to the song make *more* sense in the narrative, or did it inhibit the drama from moving onwards?

Similar important questions were raised by the order and positioning of the songs, which caused some controversy amongst viewers. *Must* the songs and events be presented in the order originally written down, or is it acceptable to shift, cut and reorder material? A very recent example of this question was posed by a production of Shakespeare's play *Hamlet*. In the theatre performance that was eventually to be filmed and relayed to cinemas throughout the country, Benedict Cumberbatch, who was playing the role of Hamlet, spoke his most famous speech beginning with the words 'To be or not to be' at the very start of the play instead of in its normal place well on in the text. Audiences and critics were outraged, but audiences coming to the play for the first time appeared to accept this change without question. Yet, such was the furore by those who felt cheated or even insulted by the change that the director reinstated the speech in its more normal position. However, the same critics who brought about this change of mind had probably reviewed countless productions of plays and musicals in which speeches and numbers had been cut or altered in less obvious ways.

Record your thoughts on the questions raised so far, and provide any examples you can think of.

Music

It is often by getting to know the tunes from a show that we first become aware of a musical. Indeed, there have been many examples in which production companies have released recordings of key songs from a musical in order to promote the show in advance of its stage opening. But there is much more to a musical than a string of memorable tunes, and if you are going to be performing one or more musical numbers in a production, you need to understand what you are doing and why you are doing it. Whatever role you have been assigned to perform – whether it is as an anonymous member of a chorus or as a named person in the drama – you are a 'character' with emotions, dilemmas, motives, dreams, attitudes and a personal story, all of which are expressed and explored through music.

Before you begin to learn any songs that you may have to sing, think about the 'Overture' to the entire show. What does it tell the audience? How does it prepare them for what is to follow? How does the opening music relate to what you may have to do later? Does it, for example, hint at one of the songs you will sing or establish a mood to which your character might respond?

Now think about the song(s) you have to sing. What are you saying and to whom are you saying it? Why do you sing rather than speak? How does the singing of a particular song move the narrative of the work onwards? Do not even consider learning the notes until you can answer these questions.

Drama

Any musical is a type of play that tells a story. You must fully identify with that story as an essential part of your preparation. Where does your character fit into the narrative? What is your character trying to achieve, and how will you convey that to an audience? How does your character relate to the other characters in the drama? Make a checklist of all the characters, and then note your character's relationship with and attitude towards them.

Now think about the shape of the drama: where are its climaxes and releases of tension? Where are the explosions of energy and moments of quieter reflection? If you cannot answer such questions, you cannot make a valuable contribution to the whole because you have not understood what the work is attempting to communicate.

As you think about the drama, consider also the way in which your director has chosen to stage it. What scenery, décor and costume decisions have been made? What will you be wearing and why? In what location is each scene of the story set and staged, and how does your character relate to that? Is, it, for example, your home town or some unfamiliar or fantastic place? How do you react to that in your performance?

It is your job as a performer to know the answers to all these questions. Never just think of the moment when you are on stage: the drama continues throughout the duration of the show, and you are an integral part of it, even if you are waiting 'in the wings'.

And finally, as part of your initial thinking, discover all you can about the inner life of your character, and consider how you might convey aspects of this life with your director's help. Explore the situations in which your character is shown, and ask yourself how these will affect her or him. Even if you spend much of the time on stage singing, remember, it is not *you* singing; it is your character, and that singing has a dramatic purpose.

Dancing

In their book *Choreographing the Stage Musical* (UK, 1987; USA, 2008) Sunderland and Pickering give sixteen possible reasons why dancing might be an important ingredient of a musical. You might like to consult this list and/or make a note of the need and reason for choreography in the box below.

Since the musical, or musical comedy as it was originally called, became an established art form, choreography has provided much more than decoration to the various works. Some musicals include incidents in which dancing is integral to the plot: for example, the dance/disco competitions in *Grease* or *Saturday Night Fever*; the dances in a night club in *Cabaret*; or ball scenes in *My Fair Lady* or *Seven Brides for Seven Brothers*. Such is the mixture of hard work, glamour, triumph and frustration that accompanies the world of dance, there are a considerable number of musicals that are set within that world: *Cover Girls*, *A Chorus Line* and *Sweet Charity* are good examples, whereas a work like *West Side Story*, probably the first musical to be directed by its choreographer, tells large aspects of its narrative through the medium of dance.

Whereas it is possible to undertake a considerable amount of private preparation for singing and acting, the tradition in dance is for the learning, devising and rehearsal to take place in a 'class' situation with some 'breakout time' for groups to work on their pieces. In this context it may at first seem difficult to inject any individuality into a performance because the emphasis may be on learning 'steps' to be carried out in unison. However, even if you are quite literally a member of a chorus line, you must have a clear idea of why you are dancing and what you hope the audience will read from your performance. It is not enough, in any performance situation, to simply learn and repeat a pattern of rhythmic movements, even if these demand expert technique and execution. You must understand precisely what it is you wish to communicate.

There is, of course, a fine line between the apparently spontaneous gestures and movements you might employ in a sung solo or duet and the moment when you might break into a tap routine or some recognised form from jazz, contemporary or ballroom dance. Such transitions will, once again, demand that you understand why your character has chosen to use this means of communication rather than speech or song.

Much of the recent interest in the study of musical theatre has come from the discipline of dance, and very high standards are now expected and achieved. The ability to move seamlessly between dancing and singing has become almost a hallmark of the musical theatre performer, but this has sometimes neglected the understanding that, in the context of theatre, this is really a form of acting in which it is vital to communicate thoughts and ideas as clearly as if they were spoken dialogue.

Once again, therefore, you must be able to justify and explain every aspect of your performance in whatever combination of singing, dancing and speaking you may be called upon to use.

3 Preparing for Performance

Using Part Three

As a student of musical theatre, you will spend a great deal in preparing for some kind of performance. This may be a simple workshop activity, short solo or an entire production. Whatever the scale of the ultimate performance, the process of preparation remains essentially the same, and it can be a lonely task. Musical theatre performers have a vast range of personal tools to bring to their work: these include vocal and physical skills, but also a set of attitudes and approaches. Understanding precisely what you are able to bring to a task is an essential preliminary to detailed work on a particular piece, and this requires some honest appraisal of your 'tools'.

In the following pages we encourage you to explore those personal and artistic factors that will shape your ability to prepare effectively, and we urge you to respond to all the suggestions and exercises in order to equip yourself to react to any demands made of you as a performer.

The activities which follow include elements of reflection and self-criticism, and we hope that you will respond honestly and carefully to the questions we have posed. At the same time, we would suggest that you adopt many, if not all, of the preparatory exercises we have described, in order to become a rounded and successful practitioner.

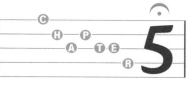

Deciding the Condition of our Tools

Performance – a state of mind

We suggest that you start by identifying the apparent demands of performance and trying to recognise your 'ideal performing state of mind.' However, to do this we need to clarify what we understand by 'performance' as there are many aspects of life which seem to be a performance or at least have performative elements.

Identify some situations where you recall having given the performance of your life – perhaps in the principal's or a professor's office, in the classroom, on the sports field, when meeting someone you love or during an incident at home.

What were the performance elements in each situation?

Compare one of these 'real-life performance situations' with a performance event (such as a stage show or carnival) that has involved you. What are the differences – if any?

Did you experience a sense of uncertainty because you were fearful of any aspect of the occasion or event?

Were you aware of any personal anxiety?

Did you ever change your mind or reconsider the way you were feeling?

If there is even a hint that you experienced some or all of the above, then you understand that to be a performer you have to be strong minded and prepared for every element of performance. There can be no room for negativity in your work. If there is, it will trigger reactions that produce mental distractions and tensions in your body. This is damaging to the ability to dance, speak, act or sing. Another result of tension is poor concentration, which has equally negative results. If you are to be successful in this performance work, you must be totally aware and confident of your own thought patterns and powers of reason.

Your level of performance is a direct result of your thinking and feeling before, during and after the event. Think of a few performance opportunities you have been given in your training where you have allowed personal distractions to prevent you from being successful. In other words, think about moments when your mental state has interfered with your performance potential.

Identify a few situations where you have allowed yourself to be distracted from performing. Give the reasons.

The following phrases might be familiar to you:

I can't perform today; I didn't get the music until yesterday.

I have been so busy with other work.

I haven't had enough time to get together with my teacher.

I have been ill this week.

I forgot we had to prepare this for today.

I am not feeling very well.

I need some water because my throat is dry.

I have a cough – can I sing next week?

I didn't understand.

I am confused! (This is an all too common phrase – avoid it at all costs. Try to work out why you feel like this.)

Have you used any of these personal excuses? If so, it is good to be aware that they are the danger signals and must be conquered before the world of performance can be fully understood. It may seem simplistic, but if we have joy in performing and understand why we are doing what we are required to do, then mental blocks tend to go away. The main problem here is that performance is hardly ever thought of as 'process', but in the minds of performers it is always associated with the final product, when, hopefully, such expressions as 'perfection', 'excellent', 'well done', and 'good job' resound around the classroom.

Mental skills have to be learned in the same way that you learn both physical and vocal techniques. Mental, movement, dance, acting and vocal skills are all learned through practice. You now have to engage with the world around you, conquer your innermost fears in order to enable performance to have a legitimate part to play in your life. So often it is the small things that can disturb you, and yet they are easy to control through careful initial thinking.

One example is what happens in the audition room. Musical theatre performers often become flustered when trying to explain to the musical director how they want the song to be played. This vital process needs to be rehearsed in much the same way as everything else.

Of course a performance can be 'good' without your having complete control over it and may be the result of inspired intention. But more often than not there is a greater chance of success if you work at the appropriate mental skills. Your aim should always be to achieve the peak performance and to create the correct climate for that to happen.

There are many fears that you might encounter during your performance career, but you might like to consider the following as a means of developing your sense of 'preparedness' for your future work:

1. Monitor the time spent on preparing for the role. How are you managing the time?
2. How do you feel about the performance work you are preparing for? You must always embrace the character's problems, not your own.

3. What strategies have you identified that enable you to deal with rehearsal or learning activities?
4. Monitor the time spent on all activities in order that you have time for yourself as well as for performance activities.
5. Aim to concentrate on the present moment rather than thinking of the consequences and future possibilities.
6. Keep positive about the work, and never be critical or dismissive of the dramatic situation being explored. Never just rehearse – perform!

The work in which you are currently engaged establishes the basis for future performance. The more understanding you possess about the areas in your performance that need improving, the more chance you have of achieving a high level every time.

Important ingredients in relation to a successful performance are **self-awareness** and **complete control**. As an actor you need to recognise your personal emotional state before and after performing. Learn to fine-tune your performance work by focusing on the appropriate critical points arising from the text or action, not on the final outcome. If you become too concerned with the final outcome, you will find it very difficult to work 'in the moment'. If this happens, you will waste energy that could have been put into the performance.

Your main aim should be to gain control over every one of your performance 'tools'. Focus on the functional vocal and breathing muscles, your emotions and thoughts in order to integrate these into a fine and joyous performance.

It is often in the studio and the rehearsal room that much of this work is developed, and we suggest that you keep particularly careful entries in your journal relating to any of the points we have considered here. Identify the following aspects of your approach to work:

1. Describe your mental state when going to class. What are you thinking?
2. Have you prepared sufficiently for this session?
3. Do you just learn the words and the music, or do you think as the character?
4. Do you often feel this work is …? (Give reasons for your answer)
   a. pointless
   b. too difficult
   c. easy
   d. repetitious
5. Do you worry about what other people are thinking, and if so, why?
6. Do you trust your teacher, professor or director?
7. Do you keep saying, 'I understand' and 'Yes, I agree' when nothing could be further from the truth?
8. Do you find it difficult to take criticism?
9. Do you become ill just before a class? How do you manage this?

When you have completed this exercise

1. Make an effort to discuss any of the above points in relation to a class, rehearsal, practice session, master class or performance event in detail with others (especially your closest friend).

2. Speak to others in your group to whom you do not usually speak. Consider how they see you and your work. You might be pleasantly surprised.

Remember that sharing your experiences, expertise and perspectives can be of immense help in developing your self-awareness. These discussions also help you to discover that there are many performers in exactly the same situation as yourself.

Overall, this work depends on the act of *preparation*.

Write down your own ideas about preparation at all levels of your performance work, and discuss your thoughts and ideas with others.

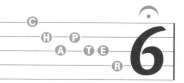

6 Sharpening our Physical and Vocal Tools

A sign on the wall of a chiropractor's office in New England says, 'You've only got one body.' It is as well to remember this as you ask your body to dance, act, sing, think and function at its best in rehearsal and performance. We make constant demands on our bodies, and every aspect of them is linked in some way. We cannot isolate the part that sings from the part that breathes or dances; we cannot think without the supplies of oxygen or chemicals transported by our blood stream. We are a single entity capable of multiple activities, and we must help that extraordinary machine to operate at its most efficient for the whole entirety of our performing lives.

Every musical theatre student should know the importance of warm-up techniques that prepare our bodies to cope with the demands of performance. In many cases you will be led in warm-up sessions by choreographers, teachers or directors of specific skills such as dance, voice or physical theatre, and most of these activities will take place in a 'class' situation. For you to achieve this, you need to take responsibility for your own learning and preparedness, and we are now providing some ideas for private practice that you should use either before or in addition to any more specialised warm-up activities. All these suggestions are intended to promote your well-being, development, and in addition prevent injuries.

Exercises for relaxation and warm-up for actors, singers and dancers

1. Start the day: YWTL

Think of a cat waking and how it stretches every limb and muscle before going into action. Stretching immediately releases stored energy and enables you to embark on an activity with a positive state of mind. Begin *every day* and *every warm-up session* with this exercise (see Figure 6.1):

1. Stand with your arms raised above your head in a Y shape, thumbs facing backwards and head slightly tilted back. (Please take caution with this head tilt.)
2. Stretch upwards while *squeezing the shoulder blades towards each other* and squeezing the buttocks. Hold for a count of ten.
3. Repeat with your arms in a W shape, your hands level with your ears.
4. Repeat with your arms in a T shape.

Figure 6.1 *(a),(b),(c),(d). YWTL*

5. Repeat with your arms in a shape of two Ls, your hands and elbows level with your waist.

Your power supply is now fully switched on.

2. Complete relaxation with a mantra to memorise

Before embarking on a more extensive 'warm-up' it is important to eliminate all tension from your body. If you retain tension, the exercises will be counter-productive. After your initial stretching follow this simple routine (see Figure 6.2):

Lie on your back with your head supported by a book or small cushion. Bend your knees and ensure that your feet are flat on the floor and your arms are lying comfortably by your side. This is the 'Alexander position', often referred to as 'constructive rest' by practitioners and used as a resting position for all work with the Alexander technique.

As you lie quietly, try to empty your mind of all concerns, and then whisper the words '*freer, softer, more relaxed*' over and over again, and feel your body

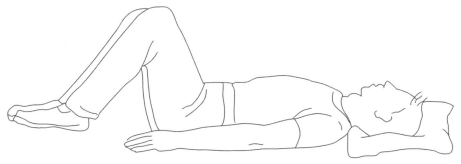

Figure 6.2 *Complete relaxation*

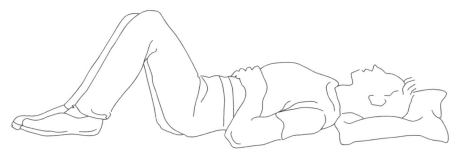

Figure 6.3 *Navel to spine*

responding by apparently sinking deeper into the floor. This position gives the feeling of providing energy to the spine.

Remain in this position for several minutes.

3. Deep breathing: navel to spine

It is no coincidence that the word 'breath' has the same origins as the words 'spirit' and 'inspiration', because breath lies at the root of everything we attempt. Always ensure that you have a good *supply of fresh air* before embarking on any breathing exercises: so many students overlook this obvious but vital factor (see Figure 6.3).

Remaining in the 'constructive rest' position, place your hands gently on your abdomen. Now take a deep, slow breath through your nose (inhale), expanding your chest. Hold your breath for a count of three.

Now slowly breathe out through your mouth (exhale) and imagine your navel sinking in until it almost reaches your spine. As you do this, make the

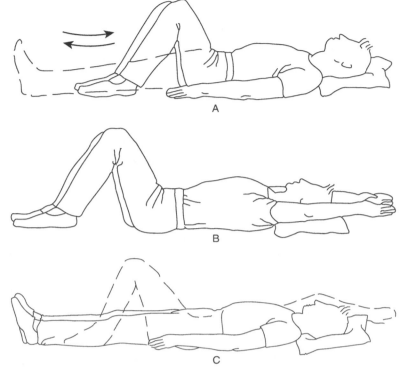

Figure 6.4 *(a),(b),(c). Synchronising breath and movement*

sound 'ha' on your breath, and make it last for a count of three. Be sure to feel your abdomen rising and falling as you inhale and exhale, and don't be afraid to let your abdomen expand. This will not create a permanently large belly; on the contrary, it will help tone your abdominal muscles.

Repeat this sequence at least ten times.

4. Synchronising breath and movement

Breath is not a separate entity from movement or vocalisation: it is an integral part of all activity. The following exercise will help you to experience the holistic nature of physical action, tune your body and prepare you gently for more demanding action (see Figure 6.4).

Remain in the 'constructive rest' position, breathing deeply. As you exhale, slide your left foot until your left leg is lying straight on the floor. As you inhale, bring the same leg back to its original bent position with the foot flat on the floor. As you exhale again, repeat the process with the right leg. Continue to move each leg, in turn, in time with your breathing. As you breathe *out*, the foot moves away from the centre of your body; as you breathe *in*, it moves back towards the centre.

Now do the same with your arms only. As you breathe *out*, lift your right arm from its position by your side, and stretch it so that it is extended and lying flat on the floor above your head. As you breathe *in*, bring it back to lie by your side. Now repeat the process with your left arm. Continue to move alternate arms in this way for several minutes.

Finally, move your opposite arm and leg in the same way. As you stretch your left leg and right arm, breath out; as you return them to their resting position, breathe in. Repeat this with the right leg and left arm until you are moving in a smooth rhythm dictated by your breath. Relax in total stillness for a few moments when you have completed the exercise.

5. The cat for flexibility

Shoulders and limbs should now be free of tension, but now we need to prepare our spine for work. Avoid sitting up suddenly from floor exercises; roll gently onto your side to move to a new position. The following exercise is a classic yoga-based activity (see Figure 6.5):

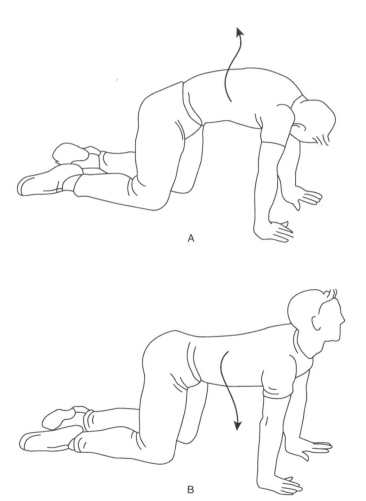

Figure 6.5 *(a),(b) The cat*

Kneel down on 'all fours', your hands directly beneath your shoulders and your back perfectly flat and your head held level, looking ahead. Now exhale slowly (still making the 'ha' sound as you do so) while you slowly round your back into an arch and let your head hang down. Hold this position and feel the gentle stretch in your back.

As you exhale, slowly hollow your back, and lift your head until it is looking up. Again, feel the gentle stretch in your abdomen as you move.

Now move between these two opposing positions for several minutes, aiming to move a little deeper and stretch a little more fully as you progress.

6. Repose and gather

Before leaving floor-based exercises, we need to gather our energy and find an ideal position for repose. Move into this directly from 'the cat' (see Figure 6.6):

Sit back on your haunches, and allow your arms to hang loosely by your sides.

Now flex gently forwards, rounding your back, until the top of your head is resting on the floor just in front of your knees. Allow your arms to lie gently on the floor on either side of your curled-up body. Breathe comfortably, deeply and slowly.

After a while, roll carefully onto your side and stand up slowly, ready to work on your posture and movement, but return to this position whenever you feel the need.

7. Developing good posture (another mantra)

As you will discover when you undertake exercises specific to dancing, singing and acting, the importance of appropriate, balanced posture cannot be exaggerated. Try to get into good habits by following this simple process (see Figure 6.7):

Stand straight with your weight equally balanced between both feet.

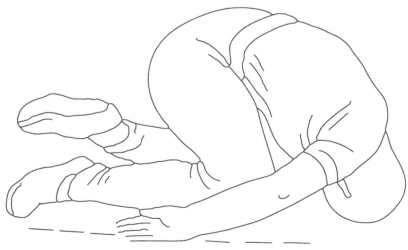

Figure 6.6 *Repose*

Inhale, lifting your shoulders up to your ears, and as you do so, go up onto your toes. Exhale with a 'ha!' while dropping your shoulders and bringing your feet down so that you make a good solid connection with the floor. Repeat this several times.

Now begin to walk around the room, with your head in a level position, and as you do so, whisper to yourself, *'Neck free, head lifted, back lengthens and widens'.*

Store these sensations in your body, and whenever you walk down the street or are aware of tension in your body, repeat these words to yourself. You will find that you will feel and probably be several centimetres taller.

8. Maintaining and restoring your 'C' curve

We often say of things and people that they are 'a pain in the neck' because we often perceive the neck as holding almost more tension than any other part of the body. One reason for this is that our heads are extremely heavy. At the point where the spine carries most of the weight of the head, it should curve backwards, but aspects of modern living, especially staring at computer screens, tend to make us poke our heads forwards. To maintain and restore the healthy 'C' curve and free the spine that transmits vital messages to our brains, follow these instructions (see Figure 6.8):

Figure 6.7 *Good posture*

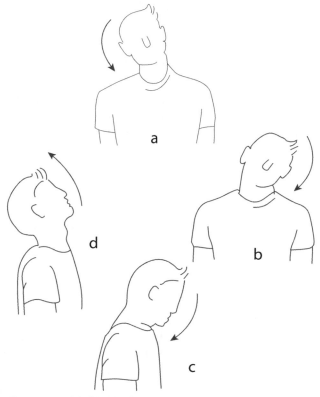

Figure 6.8 *(a),(b),(c),(d) Maintaining the 'C' curve*

Stand in a straight, balanced, relaxed posture. Ensure that there is no tension in your shoulders.

Bring your chin in towards you, and as you do, taking great care, tilt your head back gently, and hold for a count of ten.

Lower your head gently to its normal position, and then repeat the process. Hold for ten, and try to take your head back a little further each time.

Repeat this process, aiming to do this several times throughout the day to release any build-up of tension.

9. Energising the spine

The spinal cord, that carries messages to and from the central nervous system runs through the centre of the spine and is the major source of our creative energy. We need to care for our spines and keep them supple and flexible (see Figure 6.9).

Try the following, and then feel the sensation of warmth in your back:

Stand with your feet flat on the floor, shoulder width apart.

To rotate the trunk, flex your elbows up to be level with your shoulders.

Then turn alternately to the left and the right, building up momentum as you gently twist the trunk of your body.

Allow your heels to come off the floor while your toes remain on the floor, and increase the speed and momentum in a controlled manner.

Keep your head and neck aligned with your torso at all times as you twist. Gradually reduce the speed and momentum, and return to a still position.

10. Patting away the tension

It is important to remember that the body can acquire damaging and unhelpful tensions at almost any time. Here is one activity to keep as a personal remedy (see Figure 6.10):

Stand with your feet shoulder-width apart and both pointing forwards.

Take the 'lock' off your knees, and stand with your knees slightly bent. This is a position familiar to those who practice Yoga and Tai Chi.

With the wrists very loose, shake your hands and then use them to gently pat various parts of your body in turn:

The small of your back

The top of the head

The back of your neck.

Your legs and thighs

Allow your hands to move from one place to another as if they were liquid moving over the surface of your body.

Enjoy the sensation of warmth and stimulation that this brings.

Return to any of these exercises at any time. They are your constant companions.

As you have been reminded in the opening of this chapter, 'You've only got one body…' to dance, act, sing, think and function at its best in rehearsal and

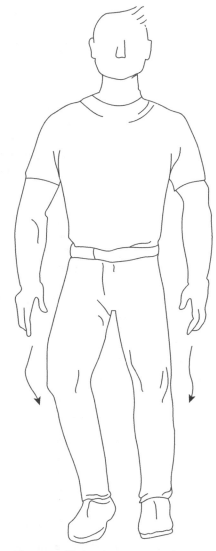

Figure 6.9 *Energising the spine*   **Figure 6.10** *Patting away tension*

performance. Having agreed this, it would be useful to identify what a performer is required to achieve in each session, rehearsal or performance in order
to gain the most effective outcome.

Being aware that we always take personal responsibility and ownership of
our own learning and preparedness, consider a few suggestions made for you
to use as a checklist at the start of each day.

Often a lack of focus and engagement is a major cause for distraction, and
this lack of engagement results in minimal progress. The physical warm-ups
already encountered are to be an essential part of your working day, and repetition of the exercises is where the essence of the work is achieved. 'Orders,

orders, orders!' and repeated aspects of rehearsal feature regularly in the lives of a performer. We must understand the nature of repetition and engage as positively as we can with this concept from the very beginning of the journey.

Personal issues should be removed from your mind. Often the embodiment of these issues is connected with an essential part of the social kit of today – the mobile phone. It is essential to realise how you interact with this technology and avoid letting it overpower and distract you in the rehearsal room. It effectively connects you to the outside and so is definitely a potent distraction in terms of your performance.

Have a look at the following list, and identify any areas that you have become aware of in your own training. You might like to add to this list and write a short sentence in your personal journal about each one and how you have dealt with these issues in both rehearsal and performance. This will also contribute to your understanding of what is research and development, and how information can be gathered to inform and understand personal growth. At a later stage in your career as both student and academic, you will be able to consider a variety of methods of collecting information and data that will contribute to your research profile and inform your study and intellectual development within the subject area.

Concentration
Focus
Confidence
Trust
Technique
Fitness/stamina

Poor concentration is often due to a lack of focus and distraction brought about by personal troubles. Rehearsal insecurity is often caused by a lack of preparation, being tired owing to a heavy personal schedule of activities after class, poor warm-up schedules and inability to listen to others in a positive manner. This sometimes leads to poor vocal projection within the rehearsal process, inevitably causing indecision within the work performed.

Identify situations where a lack of preparation has affected your own performance work.

The trick to developing confidence is to be pro-active by maintaining and keeping a personal notebook. This way you can keep an accurate record of what you have achieved and how you have progressed. All too often we forget what we have been taught, and we can be heard saying, 'We learnt nothing in the last year.' If only such students had taken the time to assess exactly what they did know and what they know now, they might understand exactly how much they have progressed. You need to be able to compare the present with the past so that you can be proud of your noted achievements.

A lack of focus and concentration can be improved by responding to the tempo of specific exercises or physical movements and engaging more fully with the overall learning process. For example, an excellent way to prepare a spoken or sung text is to perform it silently or even to hum the melody if it is a song. You will be surprised at how much you learn about the text or song and your physical well-being by completing this exercise. Another way of working is to think about the section that causes you the most trouble rather than starting at the beginning. Remember also that poor concentration or focus can be caused by dehydration, so have plenty of water to keep you going.

Aim to develop skill by skill and by doing so become secure in your performance technique. Remember, without technique there is no artistry. All too often we are in a hurry to get to the goal rather than experiencing the journey of discovery. Learn one skill at a time, and do not try to do everything. Always be aware when you have succeeded in a specific task, and note what you think worked. Overall be aware of your own feelings, and do not rely on what others think about you.

In the development of technique and retaining new skills, a good trick is to combine warm-up exercises and various vocal techniques when working and preparing on text – sung and spoken. This way you will realise the purpose and relevance of the warm-up exercise and so develop a good performing technique as well as learn new material in an effective manner. Again, it is important to relax and develop one skill at a time. It is impossible to get everything correct at once. We are often too hard on ourselves because we always think of the outcome rather than the process. Always consider the performer as an athlete and train as such.

Fitness and stamina are very important. You need to dedicate yourself to your art, and this means recognising the potential physical, mental and emotional effort required. This impacts upon your understanding of your personal nutritional intake and involves drinking plenty of water, avoiding certain foods, medicines and drinks that might impact upon your body and voice.

This brings us back to the starting point of this chapter and the importance of physical presence, posture and its impact upon the performer as actor, singer and dancer.

Breath

You will not be surprised that breath is at the centre of a performer's technique, and if this area of work is not understood in the early stages of the performer's learning, then disaster will eventually strike. Breath excites the body and empowers the mind, body and soul to communicate with the outside world (the audience). Breath is the power between the engine (lungs) and the wheels (vocal folds) of the human body.

For the purpose of this workbook we are going to concentrate on the making of a good vocal sound by the use of three basic types of vocal onset. These will give you a flexible repertoire of vocal qualities, colours and approaches for you to communicate a wide range of emotions. In much the same way as an athlete might prepare his or her specific action so the actor/singer/dancer has a specific way of preparing the onset of sound and can make decisions as how best to form the sound he or she wishes to create. This is achieved by breath meeting the closed vocal folds at differing pressures and speeds and requiring them to vibrate at various frequencies in order to create the various pitches and qualities recognised as either speech or song.

Breath is essential to life and indeed empowers us to communicate our art to the world around us. Our first sounds were made by differing qualities of breath to indicate a variety of emotions. In infancy, we are able to distinguish in the child the difference between crying, laughing and speaking. At this early stage in life, we also become aware of the different impetus of breath, and it is essential that we recall this when singing for performance. Breath for performance is about recognising that the whole body is actively engaged in order that the individual artist can express an idea that is unique and original.

If you consider the warm-up exercises at the start of this chapter, you will be aware of how breath is drawn into your body as you work through each exercise, and the release of all breath as the exercise comes to a conclusion. Once you have captured this idea of flow of breath in your physical work, you will be able to apply this to the emotional demands of a character, and so breathe life into the emotional being of your character.

Consider the following vocal exercises, and write a few words about your discoveries.

Exercise 6.1   Sing each of the notes to *Ah*. Take a breath before singing the next note.

Three notes written on stave: middle 'c', 'g' and 'd':

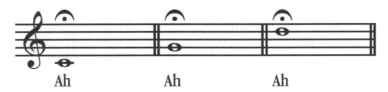

What did you notice in relation to your breath, posture and thought process?

Middle 'c'	Quite easy to sing. Nice sound, comfortable, relaxed. Free.
'g'	Slight vocal fold resistance, breath pressure changed slightly to cope with the higher pitch. Sound okay.
'd'	You might have found this top note a little more difficult to sing, perhaps feeling some tension.

If you experienced any of the sensations we have suggested, or even considered different ones, that is fine, but these three singing examples do give you an insight into how to balance the breath within your body in order to have an instrument that you can rely on in performance.

As already stated, the physical warm-up exercises have suggested that good posture is essential for this work. Needless to say, posture is also essential for the sung and spoken voice to work correctly and to be free to express emotions and feelings as required by the text.

Some words of advice

1. In the first stages of your vocal studies, do not try to rush nature.
2. Allow vocal developments to be secure and unhurried.
3. Trust your vocal teacher.
4. Try to understand what each technical term means by investigation and research.
5. Never say 'Yes, I understand', if you really don't. How will your tutors know if you are not honest with them?

Before completing some simple breathing exercises, it will be helpful to see what you observe in yourself and others.

Look at yourself in a mirror and breathe in slowly a few times. Note down all the things you notice about your postural alignment.

Now observe someone else in your class or cast to see what you observe about his or her breathing.

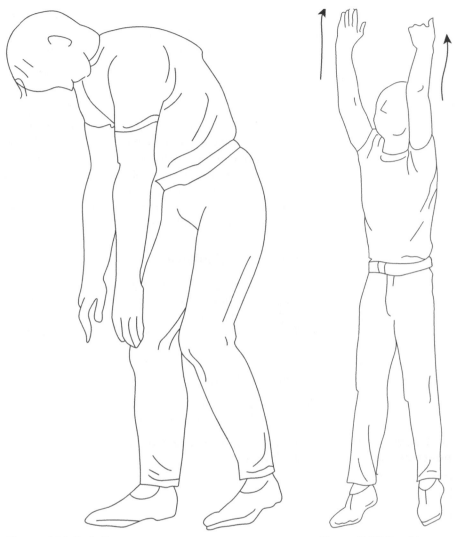

Figure 6.11 *Body flop*　　　　　　　　　　　　　　**Figure 6.12** *Reaching up*

To add to your vocabulary of warm-up exercises try the following to see how they improve your own breathing technique.

1. Bend your knees slightly, and let your upper body flop over. Inhale slowly and then exhale the breath out of your body vigorously.
2. Stand on tiptoe and reach for the ceiling with both hands. On an intake of breath, extend the right hand to reach a particular light in the ceiling while the left hand remains stretching towards the ceiling. Reverse the procedure, with the left hand reaching for the light and the right hand relaxed.

Having completed these two simple tasks, adopt a good upright posture and breathe in. Hopefully, what you now experience will demonstrate how the body is working for you as you sense a feeling of expansion within your body.

Complete observation exercises at several points within your voice studies, and notice improvements and differences in your postural alignment.

---

1. How does your breathing technique inform your vocal performance?

2. Identify any comments made by your teacher regarding this work.

It is important to remember that this is all to confirm that you are developing as both a performer and a thinker.

Having considered how important breath is to the performer, it is now essential to ensure that the throat feels in a comfortable state in order to let the vocal folds vibrate freely and enable you to make a good sound.

There are several simple exercises concerning the jaw and tongue that you should employ to help you recognise this important aspect of your work.

Look in a mirror and note the position of your jaw when you open your mouth.

Does your jaw still feel tight? Perhaps your jaw was being pulled backwards as you dropped your jaw – can you see signs of a double chin? If you noticed any of these things, a quick solution is to massage your jaw gently with your hands until it feels released. Have another look in the mirror, and you will see and feel a difference. Now consider the position of your tongue. Aim to let the tip of the tongue lightly touch the bottom front teeth – avoid pushing.

Having achieved this, try the following simple exercise, and see how it feels when speaking and then singing.

Exercise 6.2(a)   Speak Ma/Ma/Ma/Ma
Exercise 6.2(b)   Sing on any note for four counts: Ma-a-a-a/Ma-a-a-a/
Ma-a-a-a/Ma-a-a-a

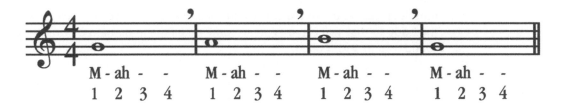

Supplement this exercise with vowels such as 'ee' and 'oo'. If this all feels comfortable, then you are prepared and ready to sing and speak.

It will always be useful to seek a second opinion from your voice teacher with regard to this work just in case you are not seeing the whole picture.

The art of singing is very much like learning to drive a car. In the beginning it is the starting and stopping that is the most complex of tasks, whereas the actual journey is less traumatic – unless an emergency stop is required at any point. However, as with driving a car, once the difficulties become second nature, you never need to consider these factors again. Remember that the somewhat bumpy ride we might experience at the beginning of our studies will soon be overcome, and the joy of singing will be an experience to be enjoyed for a very long time. Let us just consider, for the purpose of this workbook, the starting point from which the driving lesson also begins.

Before you begin the next section of work, just take a little time to answer a few simple questions about your own work and identify how much you understand about your own voice at this stage in your journey. You may have heard many of these questions before, both in class or in your individual lessons. Be your own teacher for a little while, and consider the following questions as honestly as you can.

QUESTIONS	YES	NO
Are you often told not to sing so loudly?		
Do people comment on your being a little breathy in tone?		
Do you find it difficult to sing the high notes in your songs?		
Do people comment on a lack of energy in your lower notes?		
Do you lose energy when singing a short melody or phrase?		
Are you ever told that you can't be heard?		
Do you lack clarity in articulation?		
Do you feel tiredness in shoulders and neck when you sing?		
Do you feel tension in your jaw when you sing?		

It would be very useful to show these results to your vocal tutor and work out a plan of action so that you can monitor all these points at different stages of your singing sessions. Revisit these same questions in about six months and see what has changed. Remember, always treat your voice tutor as your guide and mentor.

You have now prepared yourself and understood the importance of good posture, breath and a relaxed jaw and throat. Now you need to consider the muscles (vocal folds) that actually control and define the breath as it escapes the body so that you can explore in some detail the beginning or 'onset' of sound – sung and spoken.

The vocal folds, as a function of the human body, are multi-purpose. They act as a means to protect us from (i) choking on food as we swallow or (ii) blocking the airway and so increasing tension that enables the body to manage bodily functions such as lifting heavy objects or even giving birth. But for performers, the vocal folds hold a special role as they act as the gateway to the outer life of the performer, thus enabling sound to be transmitted in a variety of ways according to the intentions and emotions of the singer/speaker.

In the world of the sung and spoken voice, the breath is inspired by the thought and is communicated by the breath passing through the vocal folds. The actor's world in turn has to have breath, life and purpose 'off stage' before the agreed point of entrance, in order for the established 'on stage' moment and the ensuing action to have consequence and truth. If preparation of body and thought are not in existence, then our work has little or no consequence.

It is essential to understand how the vocal folds work in order for you to make decisions about your vocal work later. However, these exercises are not to be made into part of a ritual practise regime. They should become part of your normal general rehearsal work once you recognise what you are actually doing to create the sound you are trying to achieve.

To experience the *vocal fold open*, breathe in and suspend the breath for a short while before singing or speaking the vowel 'ah'.

To experience a *vocal fold closed*, go as if to cough. You will find a clear resistance to sound.

Now try to experience both *open* and *closed* vocal folds. Sing 'ah' as before, and after the count of four, just stop the sound; then after another count of four, make the 'ah' sound again.

The above exercise is only to demonstrate what it feels like to close and open the vocal folds so that you are aware of the vocal action. You will never be required to take this action whilst you are singing. *Please remember this!*

Putting it together bit by bit...

Let's use the phrase 'What do you know?'

Exercise 6.3(a)   Speak the phrase.
Exercise 6.3(b)   Sing the phrase to the melody given in 6.4, exploring the different situations and ways of communicating the phrase, especially in the rhythm and the impact of the time signatures on the meaning and feeling of the sung phrase.

Try to identify (i) how the sound is made for each of the following everyday situations; (ii) the quality of the breath; and (iii) how your body felt when speaking the phrase.

1. Telling a secret
2. Being annoyed
3. Being sad
4. Speaking at a distance or in a crowd

5. Having a conversation in a restaurant
6. Being exhausted
7. Being miserable
8. Speaking in a library
9. Being in trouble
10. Being in the classroom

You probably noticed that some of the qualities were a little breathy, for example 'telling a secret'; other situations were a little harsh and aggressive, for example 'being annoyed'; whereas 'conversation in a restaurant' was probably quite calm and direct both physically and vocally.

Try the following two contrasting phrases in a variety of the above situations to see how this impacts upon the style of singing and vocal quality. : 'If I loved you' and 'I am so sad'.

Exercise 6.4(a)

Exercise 6.4(b)

Exercise 6.5(a)

Exercise 6.5(b)

Did you notice that when you spoke with an angry delivery, your abdominal muscles were a little tight? How did your body react when you were miserable or sad? Did your body seem to lack energy and 'get up and go'?

Try to analyse each situation to see how the voice, body and breath are affected in each one, spoken and sung.

Whatever your discoveries, you will have noticed that there were different bodily and vocal responses to the words spoken and sung. You now need to secure these so that you can always make the appropriate sound to communicate the intention of the thought and situation.

Remember what was said about driving a car? At least if we get into first gear and start the car moving (onset/action), the rest can develop later, provided that we are able to find the brake to stop at some point.

Before we begin the last aspect of this chapter, you should note that many voice techniques and methods have laid claim to specific technical terminology to suit specific methods of teaching, so you will need to be aware of vocabulary used in relation to breath.

For example, in the world of the early classical singers, the original Italian term *attaco del suono* ('attack of the sound') indicated the idea of an attack on the vocal folds and may appear a somewhat harsh term for our present understanding of the word. However, originally the term was meant to indicate that the outflow of breath and the folds coming together should happen at the same time – simultaneous onset.

Let us now experiment with our own voices and experience each onset in turn.

Aspirate onset is recognised by its breathy tone. Think of the word 'help'. Now sound just the 'h' of 'help' on the breath to a count of 2, and then add the rest of the word for a further 2 counts. This is breathy in quality and is excellent when considering soft intimate ballads, sexy numbers or some elements of popular music or jazz.

Glottal onset/attack is recognised by its restricted tone. Remember the exercise to find the closed vocal fold (see above). This needs to be considered carefully as a vocal quality.

Simultaneous/balanced onset is recognised by its balance of both tone and tension in the body. A simple way of recognising the impact of this sound is to whisper 'ah' for two counts and then, without readjusting the vocal position, continue to sing the same vowel sound for a further two counts. Remember at all times to monitor the effort used when whispering and singing. They should always be the same. This is the feeling you need to experience when singing.

Having read all the above comments, do consider the following exercises as they will improve your technique and general vocal work. It is a long journey, and there are many facets to this work, but these basic ideas will hopefully provide you with interesting vocal examples.

Ten exercises to develop onset – spoken and sung

Balanced onset

Speak: M-AY; M-AY; M-AY; M-AY
Sing: Try to let the 'M' slide smoothly into the 'AY' on the second beat.

Exercise 6.6
Moderato

Hint: *Start and release each sound in the above exercise. Aim to bring a slight pause between each sung note.*
Remember to take a breath between each note

Exercise 6.7

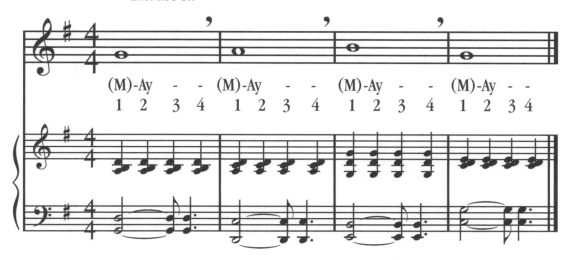

Hint: *Note that the 'M' is in brackets. Think the 'M', but don't vocalise it. Sing 'AY' for four beats.*
Note the feeling of engagement and support when you think the 'M' but sing the vowel sound 'AY.

Exercise 6.8
Andante

May may may may   May may may may   May may may may   May may may.

Hint: *When you have completed the above exercise a few times, try for some variety: replace the 'm' with 'd' (day); 'b' (bay) and finally 'z' (zay).*

Exercise 6.9
Andante Moderato

Ay   ay   ay   ay   Ay   ay   ay   ay   Ay   ay   ay   ay   Ay   ay   ay.

Hint: *If you find the above exercise difficult to sing (especially in the upper register), try the vowel sound 'ah' instead. This might make it a little easier to start with.*

Exercise 6.10
Andante Moderato

Ah   ah   ah   ah   Ah   ah   ah   Ah   ah   ah   ah   Ah   ah   ah
ay   ay   ay   ay   Ay   ay   ay   ay   ay   ay   ay   Ay   ay   ay
Oh   oh   oh   oh   Oh   oh   oh   Oh   oh   oh   oh   Oh   oh   oh

Exercise 6.11
Andante

Ah ah ah ah ah ah ah ah
Ay ay ay ay ay ay ay ay   *sim.*
Oh oh oh oh oh oh oh ay

Aspirate 'soft' onset

Exercise 6.12(a) Speak slowly: HA, HA, HA, HA; HE; HE; HE; HE; HAY, HAY, HAY, HAY.

Exercise 6.12(b) Sing carefully, making sure there is a definite silence between each note sung. We call this 'staccato' (short and detached).

Exercise 6.12(c) Now try singing the exercise legato (smoothly)

Exercise 6.13   For fun – truly have a laugh! This exercise will develop your vocal agility and improve your vocal technique.

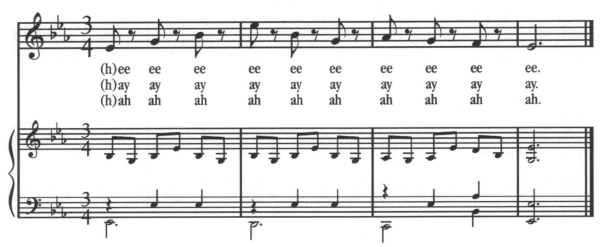

(h)ee	ee	ee	ee	ee	ee	ee	ee	ee	ee.
(h)ay	ay	ay	ay	ay	ay	ay	ay	ay	ay.
(h)ah	ah	ah	ah	ah	ah	ah	ah	ah	ah.

Glottal 'hard' attack

Exercise 6.14(a)   Speak the phrase 'Uh! Oh! Something's up!'

Exercise 6.14(b)   Sing 'Uh Oh!' on any set of five notes.

Exercise 6.14(c)   Now sing the exercise below for a few minutes only. Be careful not to push too hard.

Uh! Oh! Uh! Oh!   Uh! Oh! Uh!   Uh! Oh! Uh! Oh!   Uh! Oh! Uh!

Exercises to explore your understanding of onset

Hint: *Aim to experiment with all three onsets and have some fun with your own vocal sound. What decisions did you make and why?*

Exercise 6.15

Please note when singing this exercise that there is often a temptation to slide the words 'I' and 'am' together, thus singing 'yam' rather than 'I am'. Take care.

Exercise 6.16

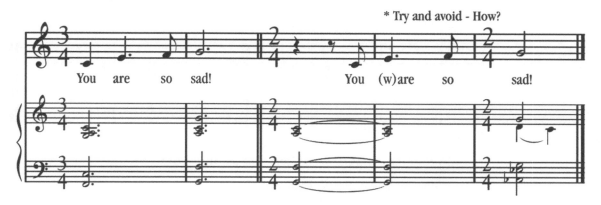

Please note when singing this exercise that there is often a temptation to slide the words 'you' and 'are' together thus singing 'ware' rather than 'You are'. Take care.

Hint: *In the following exercises it would be useful to try to analyse how you make each sound and what impact it has on both you and the listener. This will make you a more creative and inspirational performer. Make decisions and know why you make them.*

Exercise 6.17

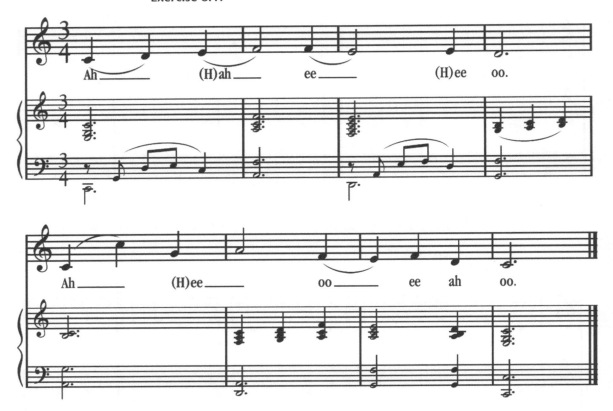

Consider the following when singing the above exercise:

1. *Analyse how you make each sound.*
2. *Analyse the impact each sound has on you whilst singing the exercise*
3. *Analyse the impact each sound might have on the listener.*

Exercise 6.18

Exercise 6.19

Remember it is essential that at all times you consult with your voice tutor in order that you keep on the right path.

Now invent your own exercises and have some fun experimenting with these simple but essential vocal qualities.

Breathing and dancing

As we have seen, breath is important for all performers and their performance lives. There is, however, some uncertainty about the role of breath in the discrete training and education of the three separate disciplines: acting, singing and dance. Yet, in their important book *The Language of Dance* (1975), Wigman, Sorrell and Rudolph speak of breath as the mysterious great master who reigns unknown and unnamed behind all and everything – who silently commands the function of muscles and joints. (p. 11)

Similarly, Leah Bartal and Nira Ne'eman in *Movement Awareness and Creativity* (2002) agree that:

a good posture produces good breathing and good breathing will produce good posture. (p. 39)

In this chapter, we have introduced you to (i) warm-up exercises that are of relevance to acting, singing and dancing and (ii) basic principles of breath for voice and for the work of the actor, singer and dancer. In fact, it becomes obvious that everything associated with performance is dependent on the basic physical skills acquired by an actor in training, whether these are aspects of posture, movement or voice.

However, we now need to think more specifically about breath for dancers and what it might mean for their training in musical theatre.

We often speak of the 'triple threat', and at the heart of this work you need to remind yourself that breath is equally important to all three disciplines. In choreography young training dancers are often required to achieve set moves and routines that demand technique, concentration and focus to 'nail the movement' as quickly as possible. One of the dangers of this is that dancers concentrate on learning the moves but physically and facially 'tighten up' in order to deliver them with precision. Thus, in the early stages of their development there is a tendency to give little attention to the *thought* behind the execution of the movement. An overall focus on the accuracy of taught movements restricts breath. As a result, the moves are presented in an effective and technical manner. The desire to be technically secure sometimes negates the creative and artistic dimension. We need to remember that, as Barbara Mettler (2011) expresses it in her online paper *The Nature of Dance*, 'A central rhythmic coordinator in all natural body movement is breathing.'

In discussion with the authors, David Ashley, a West End dancer working with Gillian Lynne on the staging of the song 'Old Deuteronomy' from *Cats*, identifies the moment when Lynne described the choreography of the arms circling upwards as 'a great big bundle of joy'. He goes on to explain that it was essential for him to lead into the movement with an inward breath and finish the movement with exhalation. In other words, a breathing pattern was established to achieve both clarity of movement *and* thought. This illustrates how important an understanding of breath is to the creative world of a dancer. It is the application of good breath control that, just as for an actor or singer, enables a dancer to identify the story to be told. David Ashley continues by suggesting that in the same way, 'freeing up the actor to truly inhabit a role is to connect the thought to the breath which then leads the impulse and intention through the actions of the active body'. The same applies to a singer or dancer.

A dancer can have beauty and technical prowess, but the real impact of breath takes place when he or she engages with the audience to convey the narrative. In any work of musical theatre, the most inspirational aspect of a performance is the evident understanding of the entire company that they must communicate the narrative and mood of every moment. All too often we see technically flawless performances that fail to engage us with the emotional content of the story.

If you, as an actor, want to be at the centre of performance work, you must understand that breath enables you to convey the truth and impulse of the action and to speak or sing the text. Breath provides the energy for both physical and vocal work. We hope that this workbook will encourage you to realise the importance of breath to all performers. Breath is an essential ingredient that enables a dancer to be effective as artist and communicator.

Remember that when dancing or learning a new dance technique or routine, we are frequently too aware of what we don't know and how we look to others, so we might retreat to the back of the dance studio. This insecurity in our work impacts on our breath. Because we concentrate on getting the movement precise and correct, we hold our breath in determination and by doing so, hold huge amounts of tension in our bodies.

You will notice that when you are working in an ensemble in a more relaxed atmosphere, you will laugh at yourself and feel a sense of fun. As a result, your breath immediately releases, and you become free and full of expression. You can now communicate to others the joy of the situation.

Now participate in the following exercises, and see how your own work is affected by the quality of your breath.

Look at 'The Jets' Song' and 'The Rumble' or 'Somewhere' from the film version of *West Side Story*. Compare and contrast their specific dance qualities, and identify how the narrative is achieved through the dance.

Make notes on the use of breath, voice and physicality within each dance sequence.

Identify and perform a short sequential pattern from a recent dance routine that you have been working on. Comment on the quality of your breath, where and when you take breath and how important this is in enabling you to achieve the best results.

Look at other dance routines from musicals on film, and with a partner work on a specific 'moment' in a routine.

Consider the following:

(i)   the actual process of achieving the perfection of each movement;
(ii)   the stage in the process when the quality of breath was considered;
(iii)   how much difference there was to your actual performance when breath was empowered by thought to add meaning, intention and a driving force to the action.

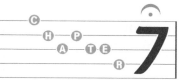

Sharpening our Mental Tools

Three essential qualities

Success in musical theatre depends on what we bring to the process of developing our skills and understanding. We have considered the idea that, as a student, you will need to acquire a high level of performance skill, but in whatever aspect of musical theatre that may be, the task will be greatly influenced by the level of **energy, curiosity** and **imagination** that you employ.

Energy

We are most aware of energy when we feel that we do not have enough. In reality energy is an essential life force that enables us to focus on a task and bring it to a successful conclusion. We often waste our energy in pointless activity, and we need to develop techniques to both conserve and maximise our energy so that we can take all our work to a higher level. This applies to many aspects of our lives as performers. As human beings we are, in fact, surrounded by many forms of energy, and it is possible to tap into these forces so that our own energy is moderated and well used.

In the ancient Indian text *Bhagavadgita*, we are introduced to a tradition known as the Vedic system, in which the nature of energy in the universe we inhabit is explored. The 'Guna' idea (which comes from the Sanskrit word for 'energy' or 'force') suggests that there are three kinds of energy:

1. **Sattva** sustains, nourishes and illuminates, bringing understanding, peace and stillness. It heightens consciousness and is concerned with light and clarity.
2. **Rajas** is concerned with movement, force, power, activity, change, drive and growth.
3. **Tamas** is the energy that regulates, sustains and maintains. It is concerned with inertia, restraint and discipline, and brings us to a state of rest.

Describe which of these aspects of energy is predominant for you at this moment.

Each of these forms of energy is present in every situation, but one of them will predominate. The difference in our experience lies in the *balance* of the energies; so, for example, Tamas predominates at night, when things are brought to rest, whereas in the early morning or evening there might be a predominance of Sattva. However, for students engaged in the demanding world of musical theatre, it is important that, instead of being like most people and wavering between Tamas and Rajas, you find ways of increasing your Sattva energy. This will not only bring a new sense of balance to your life but will also enable you to respond to the wide variety of challenges you will encounter. In order to do this, we would recommend that you build in periods of quiet reflection into your day, and always make time for a pause between activities. You may wish to get back in touch with your senses through forms of meditation or by simply listening to sounds or heightening your awareness of touch or taste. It is the Sattva that makes you a truly reflective person.

Curiosity and imagination

Teachers long for their students to demonstrate a sense of curiosity and imagination. It is through these qualities that all great discoveries have been made and every great work of art created. Musical theatre demands these qualities in abundance, and if you are not constantly enquiring into areas previously outside your experience or conceiving of a situation that is different from what you currently know, you will remain an uninspired and ineffectual worker.

Describe how you might show a sense of curiosity and imagination in learning a new song from a musical.

With a refreshed concept of curiosity and imagination, you will be able to undertake one of the most rewarding and vital aspects of our work: research.

Researching musical theatre

If you are preparing to perform or helping someone else to perform in an item of musical theatre, it is essential that you bring extensive knowledge and understanding to the task. You may simply be preparing a song from a show or undertaking a major role in a production, but in either case you will need to engage in some kind of 'research' in order to ensure that your work has depth and truthfulness. It is perfectly true that it is possible to 'perform' without much research so long as you know the words or moves and can sing the right notes, but there is *much* more to performance than that. If your work remains at the level of accurate notes, dance steps and words, it will inevitably be superficial, and you and your audience will soon become bored and frustrated.

Research can take many forms. It is now recognised that a good deal of learning and discovery takes place during the process of rehearsal and practical experiment. Such 'practice as research' is a vital part of your work, and it is important that you try to discover something new every time you engage with a piece of musical theatre in private work, lessons, group rehearsals or performance.

However, it is highly likely that you will need to supplement your research by reading and/or going to the Internet. To demonstrate how you might go about this form of research and what it might yield, we are going to provide you with an example of the learning and enrichment that can be achieved by research-ing a topic. The most important factor to remember in this activity is to *make connections* between the various facts and ideas you discover in order to move forward.

Let us imagine that you have developed a special interest in sound record-ings of songs from shows and that you are particularly fascinated by the musical comedy *Show Boat* with music by Jerome Kern and lyrics by Oscar Hammerstein II. *Show Boat* was first performed just after Christmas in 1927 and was recognised as a ground-breaking piece of theatre for reasons that you will need to discover. Suppose that in your research you establish that a very popu-lar recording of one of the songs from the show, 'Ol' Man River', was made by Bing Crosby very shortly after the first stage productions.

It is quite possible that you or your students have never heard of Bing Crosby or that he is regarded as irrelevant and belonging to the generation of grandparents or even great-grandparents. But in fact he was probably the most successful popular entertainer in the West during the last two centuries. He appeared in countless movies, TV and radio shows, and he performed live all over the United States in what was known as **vaudeville** and made hundreds of popular recordings, including what remains the bestselling 'single' of all time, the song 'I'm Dreaming of a White Christmas'.

Items on display at Gonzaga University, United States (where one of the authors of this book was a professor), give fascinating details of the career of their most famous alumnus, and these are supplemented by Gary Giddings's biography of Bing (2001) *A Pocketful of Dreams*. From such sources we discover that compared to those stars of the modern music world who need to prop up their flagging careers with appearances on 'reality' TV shows, Crosby's career lasted an entire lifetime, and he accumulated a vast financial fortune. *So what was the secret of his success?*

In order to answer this question and to discover the particular reasons for the impact of his recording of 'Ol' Man River', we need to explore other aspects of Crosby's life, the times in which he was living and the context of the song from *Show Boat* that he so effectively popularised.

Bing Crosby was a student at Gonzaga University in Washington State in the Inland Northwest of the United States. Gonzaga is a Jesuit Catholic University that required (and still does) all students to follow an initial core of compul-sory subjects which included theology and elocution (what we would now call 'speech'). Being a religious foundation, worship and music were an integral part of University life, and Crosby also took courses in theatre. All these factors were to affect his development as a performer and entertainer. Bing was an outstanding student of public speaking and rhetoric, an active singer in chapel and a very enthusiastic participant in student drama. It is little wonder there-fore that he eventually became known for his impeccable diction, his ability to shape vowels and phrases, his comic timing, acting ability and his feeling for melody and mood in music. Prior to becoming a student, Bing had embarked on a career in entertainment as a member of a singing group and later became part of a successful duo touring theatres throughout the United States, but his work in this field was initially in conflict with his parents' wishes for him to study law. After several years Bing abandoned his University studies, determined to follow his dream, but some vital foundations had been laid: we shall return to those later.

When Crosby embarked on his career as a singer and entertainer, a number of key factors impacted his development. It is difficult for us to imagine it now, but he and his colleague initially performed in theatres by singing through handheld megaphones. The microphone as we would recognise it was yet to be invented, but by 1927 crude carbon mikes were replaced by the condenser mike, and Bing Crosby became its most brilliant exponent. Indeed, he virtually invented a new, intimate style of singing, using a microphone and employing careful and relaxed phrasing that came to be known as 'crooning'. Obviously, the implications of this for sound recording were considerable. At the same time, the popular music world was being transformed by the influence of African American 'blues' and 'swing' that were introduced by jazz musicians such as Louis Armstrong and taken up by influential band leaders who, at that time, had control over the tastes and styles of much popular music. The newly-perfected microphone provided the basis for far better sound recordings and ensured the growing popularity of radio, which would eventually become the medium whereby sound recordings would achieve success or otherwise. Bing Crosby's solo career was greatly boosted by his appearance on radio shows, and his emerging, unique style became familiar to thousands in his unseen audience.

What else can we discover about this 'style' that achieved such fame and success?

When Bing's recording of 'Ol' Man River' was released, Johnny Mercer, one of the leading arrangers and popular musicians of his day, remarked, 'It seemed to me he employed a completely new and different style which sounded more natural and effortless than any I'd ever heard' (quoted in Giddings, 2001, p. 169).

And in Britain Alistair Cooke exclaimed:

Word ran through the English underground that a genuine jazz singer – and a white man – had appeared in the unlikeliest place. (Ibid)

In fact, although Crosby expressed some satisfaction with his recording, he was never entirely content with his performances and went on developing and refining his unique style to the end of his life. Among other factors influencing his performance style was the cultural heritage of his Irish roots and particularly his use of the 'upper mordent'. The mordent is a broken-note decoration in music in which the performer briefly touches a higher (the upper mordent) or lower note (the lower mordent) than the main note he or she is singing or playing. This technique is particularly characteristic of Scottish and Irish folk music, and so skilfully did Crosby employ it that what became known as 'the Crosby cry' was recognised as one of his signature vocal techniques. Underlying

Crosby's approach to singing was the fact that in Irish and African American culture people expected to dance while they were singing, and whenever you listen to a Crosby recording, you feel that he has absorbed these cultures to such an extent that his performance is infused with the rhythm and sense of movement of a dance.

In the first half of the nineteenth century, Bing Crosby's maternal great-grandfather was one of several million citizens of Ireland who escaped famine and poverty to cross the Atlantic in search of a new life. When a future genera-tion of the family moved to the city of Spokane in the Northwest in 1906, Bing was already, as a child of three, constantly surrounded by music. His father, Harry, had purchased one of the first wind-up phonographs, which played cylin-ders of music through a bell-shaped horn, and when his father had replaced the cylinder machine with one that played platters, the house was full of the sounds of John McCormack (a famous Irish tenor), the Scottish music-hall performer Harry Lauder and the remarkable Jewish singer, Al Jolson. This was some twenty years before the invention of radio, and Bing was apparently mesmerised by these performers and knew all the songs by heart. (Giddings, 2001, p. 37)

The Irish were only one set of immigrants to the United States in the nine-teenth and early twentieth century, for they were joined by millions of Jewish people from parts of Europe where they had been subjected to persecution and violence. These immigrants included leading musicians from the opera houses of Vienna, Prague, Budapest, Moscow and other major cities, and they brought with them skills of performance and composition in light opera and classical music as well as their own brand of deeply held emotion in song and dance. Musical theatre as we now know it owes a huge debt to these remarkable musi-cians and their families. Bing Crosby absorbed and modified many characteris-tics of Jewish music in his own performances.

Bing Crosby's vocal techniques were, however, never divorced from the demands and meanings of the song he was singing: his approach *always* served the needs of the song, however distinctive his rendering. He seemed to dig deeply into what the composer and librettist were wishing to say and then made it his own as he shared it with and communicated it to his audience. His approach to 'Ol' Man River' was a wonderful example of this and represents one of many things we can learn by thinking about this process. 'Ol' Man River' was not an obvious choice of song for Crosby to record: it was originally conceived by the composer Jerome Kern for the very deep bass voice of the black singer Paul Robeson, although it was actually sung by another deep bass, Jules Bledsoe, in the stage premier of *Show Boat*. Fortunately for our research purposes, we still have valuable **primary sources** in the form of first-hand ver-bal accounts of what happened at the initial recording by Bing on 11 January 1928. Bill Challis, the young orchestral arranger responsible for the backing of Bing's song, was pleased to hear him sing the song an octave higher and remarked:

> He could do that and make it sound good. He had good intonation. Took the whole tune and went right on up. You didn't have to tell him what to do, he just did it and did it nicely. (Giddings, 2001, p. 170)

As a music historian, Giddings tell us that, unlike many popular performers of his day, Bing Crosby used a chest tone approach, making full use of his diaphragm:

> His vocal mask was complete and mature. But his most extraordinary gift was to communicate naturally. While other pop singers employed ponderous or flaccid tones, Bing sang the same way he spoke. His style avoided the mannerisms of style; his art seemed artless, even effortless. (p. 172)

We have established, then, that much of the success of the recording of 'Ol' Man River' was due to Crosby's remarkable and innovative vocal technique; but that is only part of the picture. In order to complete our investigation, we need to return to the work itself, *Show Boat*. If you consult one of the many histories of musical theatre (e.g. Ganzl, 1994; Kenrick, 2010; or our previous *Workbook*, 2013), you will discover that *Showboat* opened at the Ziegfeld Theatre on Broadway in 1927. If you have studied any aspect of the history of musical theatre, the name 'Ziegfeld' will already make an important connection in your thinking because the impresario Florenz Ziegfeld was best known for his 'Follies', a form of entertainment and pure escapism that invariably began with a dance routine performed by a row of glamorous white girls with uniform smiles and long legs. Such 'revues' were the main diet fed to American audiences in the early years of the twentieth century. Audiences attending the first performance of *Show Boat* immediately recognised that they were in a totally different world. The stage was filled with workers, many of them African Americans, shifting and carrying cargo and cotton bales on a waterfront. Scenes that took place on the boat told a far from glamorous story of life in the entertainment business, and the relationships and situations were tense, difficult and remarkably 'real'. This was a drama about real life in America: its joys, hardships, racial prejudices and warm humanity. A new form of music drama had been born.

The song 'Ol' Man River' weaves its way through the show, perhaps as a reminder that time moves constantly on and that, whatever people do, some things remain the same. So important is this song, sung by Joe, one of the stevedores, that it is reprised twice during the course of the action after its initial appearance during the opening scene. It is a slow, reflective ballad with a haunting melody, and the solo voice is joined by a chorus as it mounts to a climax. That climax is not only achieved through the music: it is the marriage of a memorable tune with unforgettable words, and those words would have been familiar to Bing Crosby in another context:

> Ah gets weary
> An' sick of tryin'
> Ah'm tired of livin'
> An' skeered of dyin'

The former student of theology at a Jesuit University might well recall the words of St Augustine in his *Confessions*: 'thoroughly tired of living and extremely frightened of dying' (4.6), so skilfully adapted into the lyrics of the song by Oscar Hammerstein II. Bing Crosby, on the surface an easy-going man with few troubles, concealed depths of emotion that often only emerged in song. He related to this song on a musical, verbal and philosophical level and, by so doing, had the first major recording success of his career. Like the show itself, which brought events up to date in 1927, Crosby had become the voice of a new America and would soon conquer both sides of the Atlantic.

This example of a research topic is intended to give you some indications of the means by which you can extend your knowledge and understanding of your work: now apply some of its principles by responding to the following suggestions and questions:

Research activities

1. List five factors which you believe contributed to the success of Bing Crosby's recording of 'Ol' Man River'.
2. Underline ten facts mentioned in this section that need to be connected to explain Crosby's approach to singing.
3. What have you learned about Crosby's technique that might improve your own practice?
4. Download various versions of the song we have been discussing, and compare the approaches of Paul Robeson, Bing Crosby and others.
5. Why was *Show Boat* a landmark in the development of musical theatre?
6. What other works of musical theatre explore the world of entertainment?
7. How would you explain the use of the mordent in singing?
8. What cultural influences converged in the United States during the late nineteenth and early twentieth centuries to create new forms of performance?
9. All the facts mentioned in this section of our book can be obtained from books or the Internet. Conduct your own search around the topic to see what else you can discover and how you might make connections with the facts already established.

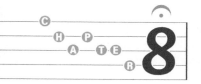

Exploring the Context of a Song and the Creation of a Dramatic Role

Researching a role and a song

In the previous chapter, we suggested that 'research' was an essential activity if the work you are preparing is to have depth and integrity. So far, we have looked at what you can learn from historical research, but it is also vital that you consider the text of the piece of musical theatre you are preparing as the most important **primary source** for research. Let us explore this idea by continuing to use the example of 'Ol' Man River' but extending the activity to *any* work you might be hoping to perform.

We would suggest that, as you look at the words you are to speak or sing, you ask yourself the following questions, all of which are crucial to the creation of a dramatic role:

1. Who am I?
2. Where am I?
3. What is happening to me?
4. What brought me to this moment?

Now, let us apply these questions to the song 'Ol' Man River' from *Show Boat*. You will need to have a copy of the show, the lyrics of the song and possibly a synopsis of the action handy at this moment. Once you have read through the lyrics by Oscar Hammerstein II several times, consider the questions we have posed.

Who am I?

This song is sung by Joe, one of the stevedores (dock workers who carry heavy loads) on board the *Cotton Blossom*, a showboat that takes cargo and entertainment to towns along the Mississippi River between the years 1897 and 1927. We see from the cast list that Joe is married to Queenie, the boat's cook, and that the song is sung early in the show and repeated twice at later stages. When the song reappears at the end of the show, Joe is thirty years older than when we first see him. We can see that the other African American workers on the boat and dockside form a chorus to provide a backing to Joe's song. From historical research we can discover that *Show Boat* was based on a popular novel by Edna Ferber and that Jerome Kern and Oscar Hammerstein II created the role of Joe especially for the well-known black actor/singer Paul Robeson, who was nearly thirty years old at the time and was, ironically, not available for the first performances.

From the speech patterns and content of the lyrics of the song, we can see that Joe is from the Deep South and is part of the culture of black gospel thought: deeply aware of colour prejudice and of the contrasts between the lives of black and white. He is thoughtful and philosophical and creates his own poetic image of the river as a wise and constant being. Joe is often shown as a reluctant worker, happier thinking than working and frequently expressing discontent with his situation. He is also a good listener, and his advice is sought by other characters. This song is initially a response to a request for advice from an aspiring performer, Magnolia, the daughter of the boat's captain. Let's consider the circumstances of the first singing of the song.

Where am I?

The stage directions tell us that Joe actually begins singing his song while sitting on a box on the dockside, idly whittling a piece of wood. We learn from the script that the *Cotton Blossom* has moored at the river dock in Natchez, Mississippi, and that Joe has gone ashore to buy flour for his wife, Queenie, who, we have already discovered, is the ship's cook. Queenie's role is usually played by a Blues singer, and we have seen her earlier 'waddling' around the stage.

It is 1887 and strict rules on racial segregation have been imposed by the white-dominated lawmakers. As Joe returns from his shopping, he is asked by Magnolia for some advice about her love life. She has fallen for Gaylord Ravenal, a handsome stranger, (who eventually turns out to be a gambler and convicted murderer) and cannot think what to do. As Magnolia goes on board, Joe and the other dock workers sing 'Ol' Man River' for the first time.

What is happening to me?

This is, of course, a far more complex question, and the answers provide the main clue as to how the song will be performed. Initially we will think of it in physical terms as to what is happening on stage, and this demands a careful reading of the stage dialogue and directions.

We have seen Magnolia on the levee (dockside) falling for Ravenal, and after they have sung a duet in which they both agree to pretend to be in love, Ravenal kisses Magnolia's hand, and 'they stand and gaze at each other'. As they do, Joe enters, carrying his sack of flour, which he places upstage centre, and he watches as Ravenal exits and Magnolia 'looks after him adoringly'. Then Magnolia becomes aware of Joe looking 'curiously' at Ravenal and asks him a direct question: 'Oh, Joe. Did you see that young man I was talking to?'

This is the first point in the drama where we become aware of Joe as a character and learn his name. Joe 'turns' and replies respectfully 'Mornin'', Miss 'Nola... Yep – I seed him – seed a lot like him on de river'. Notice Joe's speech patterns here as you prepare to sing: Joe continues to listen to Magnolia as she expresses her uncertainty about her new relationship, perhaps partly caused by his remarks. Her response is 'Oh, Joe, he was such a gentleman!', and we might imagine Joe's sceptical look as she continues: 'Have you seen Miss Julie? I got to ask her what she thinks'. She does not wait for a reply, but goes offstage, leaving Joe muttering under his breath: 'Better ask de ol' river what he thinks'. And then, he sets up the central ideas of his song as he says: 'he knows all 'bout dem boys... he knows all 'bout everythin'...' And then the stage directions tell us, 'he sits on a box, takes out a knife, picks up a (wood) shaving and starts to whittle, idly, as he sings'.

So we have established the context and physical conditions of the song, and we have gained some insights into the kind of person Joe is, but if we study the lyrics of his song, we discover that many more 'things are happening to him'.

The first few words tell us that Joe is in an unhappy situation: he would prefer to be like the river, not caring about the fact that he lives without freedom in a troubled world. The river just keeps rolling while people come and go, planting cotton or potatoes. By contrast with the river, Joe and his companions undertake gruelling physical work, constantly being ordered about and punished if they resort to drink. Joe is utterly weary of life: he does not have the emotional energy to continue, and yet he is afraid of death. At a later point in the song Joe refers to 'the Judgement Day' which, in his theology, awaits us all, so he envies the constantly flowing river that reminds us of the transitory nature of our lives in the inexorable passage of time.

More precise details of his uncomfortable situation are revealed later in the song. He paints a vivid picture of the tyranny of his white masters and the contrast between the leisured lives of the white elite and the virtual slavery of the workers. He longs to escape from this world of inequality and, using his biblical language again, longs to 'cross over Jordan' to the Promised Land. Notice how the main body of the song is repeated, and the climactic quotation from St. Augustine, which we noted in our section on Bing Crosby's rendering of the song, is emphasised by the chorus joining in:

Ah, gits weary
An' sick of tryin'
Ah'm tired of livin'
An' skeered of dyin',
But ol' man river,
He jes' keeps rollin' along!

What brought me to this moment?

If you have followed our argument so far, you will have virtually discovered the answer to this question. However, this is a complex question to ask about this particular song because it is repeated at intervals of many years throughout the show, and Joe's experiences will intensify as the action progresses. In the first instance we can safely say that Joe and his wife, Queenie, bring their somewhat resigned and philosophical attitudes to the life of the *Cotton Blossom* and that they have both survived a world of gruelling physical work and racial prejudice to which they can see no alternative.

At a later stage in the drama, we see the problems of illegal mixed-race marriages, of maintaining the 'upbeat' atmosphere needed for providers of entertainment and of disastrous personal relationships. Things do not end happily in this show, and, in contrast to many of the pieces of musical theatre that went before, *Show Boat* reveals a very dark side of American history alongside its infectious energy.

When you have studied the book and lyrics of the show carefully, you may agree with the playwright and critic Ronald Harwood (1984, p. 272) when he claims that *Show Boat* is far superior as a drama to many of the plays that were being written in the 1920s. The process we have taken you through should enable you to create a truthful role and to research your character thoroughly. We suggest that, as an exercise, you decide how you would stage and perform the three renderings of 'Ol' Man River', taking into account the four crucial questions on which this section of our book is based.

Further research activities

1. Listen to as many recorded/downloaded performances of ''Ol' Man River' as you can, and decide which show the most awareness of the character of Joe as you now imagine him.
2. Apply the four questions outlined in this chapter to a song that you are currently preparing to perform. How does this process affect your performance?
3. What are the qualities of the melody of 'Ol' Man River', and how do these reflect the situation and meanings you have been considering?
4. Joe starts to sing his song when he is sitting on a box, but what does he do for the rest of the song?
5. What other stage musicals present serious aspects of contemporary life, and how are these 'entertainment'?
6. Find other examples of dialogue that leads into a song in a stage work, and rehearse the short scene so that the dialogue flows naturally and almost imperceptibly into the song.
7. Before you even begin the process of preparing a song for performance, write a character study of the person in the drama whose words you will be using. Explain the character's age, physical situation, attitudes, relationships, aims and life experiences by reading the words he or she speaks or sings and what the person is doing.
8. Discover what kind of critical reception accompanied the first performance of the show you are working on: do you agree with what was said, and if not, why not?
9. How does the movie of *Show Boat* or of any other piece of musical theatre differ from the stage version? How might these differences affect the way you approach your work?

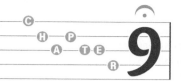

Talking with Choreographers

A great deal of debate now centres on what constitutes an appropriate dance curriculum to prepare students for the ever-changing musical theatre. As a performer this will be very important to you, and we hope that this section of the workbook, supported by practitioners from the industry, will give you some guidance as to what you really need in order to succeed.

Choreographers currently working in the West End, on Broadway and in other major cities, together with colleagues at relevant conservatoires and universities, identified the following styles as being the most useful areas of dance to study:

1. **Ballet,** an essential dance technique for all performers, whether they see themselves as actors, singers or dancers, because of its concentration on posture, for example head, shoulders, hips, legs and feet being in correct relative position to one another.
2. **Contemporary dance,** which recognizes the power of breath and narrative and so encapsulates the emotional demands of the performer.
3. **Jazz dance,** incorporating the work of Jack Cole, Jerome Robbins and Bob Fosse.
4. **Tap,** a dance technique that develops attention to rhythm and to detail of form and structure on stage.
5. **Ballroom,** in which the skills identify and express through dance and stylistic movements the emotional and physical demands of the dramatic duologue.
6. **Combat,** also considered to be a significant movement skill because of its actor-based discipline and the need to find motivations and ideas behind each movement.

Of course dance education and training must reflect the requirements for a dancer to succeed in musical theatre, but you might like to consider some of the comments made by practitioners in their conversations with us. The most important fact to emerge was that at the heart of all dance auditions was the hope that dancers had the *ability to communicate ideas and a story through movement.*

However, the choreographers understood that their role was also to enhance the aesthetic potential of a production to reach the highest possible level. So there was a responsibility for them to use their ability as teachers as well as creators to develop the performance work observed in audition.

For the hopeful performer, potential and promise go some way towards a successful audition, but there is always a danger that initial promise will not be fulfilled and will disappoint on the first day of rehearsal. Take care that you are not one of those performers who promises the world and then fails to deliver. Before we consider the responses of our choreographer colleagues in detail, we suggest that you prepare to reflect on their answers by responding to the exercises that follow:

Identify which dance styles would be required if you were going to audition for the following musicals?

Wicked
Seven Brides for Seven Brothers
My Fair Lady
South Pacific
The Sound of Music
Cabaret
West Side Story
Oklahoma!
A Little Night Music
Urine Town

Identify which of the above musicals you would currently be prepared to audition for and why.

To assist you in making decisions regarding dance areas to be studied, the choreographers to whom we spoke were asked to identify the skills they would expect at audition. Their general responses were that jazz, ballet and contemporary were the main dancing skills required, together with the ability to embrace emotions and the freedom to express ideas, intentions and thoughts.

Other thoughts to emerge from our discussions were as follows:

1. Tap was either the main skill expected at audition or not required at all. Clearly it would need to be appropriate to the style and period of musical.
2. Some choreographers suggested that if the audition panel were interested in a specific actor-singer for a role, they would find ways of dealing with their particular performance skills. Often the actor chosen would be given less challenging choreography, but at a level that would be aesthetically and technically pleasing to an audience.
3. Ballroom, mainly Latin, might be used for its potential to identify emotions, dramatic intensity and focus.
4. Commercial dance was considered useful, but often a highly specialised audition requirement.

Generally, however, our choreographers confirmed the necessity for the 'triple threat' performer to be considered the 'norm'.

When you dance or sing in a musical, you are, in fact, acting. If this is the case, then the 'triple threat' can be achieved if your acting techniques are secure and form the basis upon which all your performance work is built.

It is possible that to be a 'triple threat' does not require all skills to be at an identical high level, but an awareness of them all is certainly essential if you are to succeed in this area of performance. Do not waste time waiting for an ideal curriculum to come along to tell you what to do: it is better to 'get out there' and attend as many dance classes as possible in order to put all your skills together, even if they are not always as refined as you would wish at that moment. Monitor your own dance skills as you develop as a performer, and when you find yourself losing a potential role because of a lack of dance technique, the time has come to remedy that situation.

Remember that you are entering this profession as an individual, and although your course of study can provide you with an excellent basis, there may be particular skills that you require that are not part of your current curriculum. Search for help in the performance community in order to develop yourself as a performer and widen your potential for networking and making new contacts.

Personal dance skills audit

What are your strengths as a dancer?

What are your weaknesses?

Note a weakness, and identify how and why this should be improved.

Give yourself a time scale and a level of competence to be achieved. Take responsibility for your own learning. Identify how you are going to achieve this. Where are you going for the classes? Estimate the cost.

Remember, breath is the beginning of thought and action. By incorporating this into all aspects of performance, we can potentially achieve the status of the 'triple threat'. However, two of our choreographers, Chet Walker and Anthony Whiteman, suggest that you might now be looking to be a 'quadruple threat'. This suggests the addition of circus elements, playing an instrument or combat skills to acting, speaking/singing and dance. You might like to think how you could add these to your repertoire. You might find it helpful to look at Barbara Hartwig's responses at this point. (see p. 106)

Conversations with choreographers

We hope that by sharing these thoughts with you, you will gain a greater insight into the nature of this industry and have a clearer idea about its expectations and demands.

CHET WALKER, United States: multi-award winning director/choreographer in television, film, music video and all commercial media. Productions include 1999 Tony Award–winning musical *Fosse*; *Best Little Whorehouse in Texas*; *Annie Get Your Gun*; and *'Pal Joey'* at the Goodman Theatre, Chicago. Most recent productions include *Feelin' in the Mood*; *Sweet Charity* and *The Lady Scrapbook*.

What are the qualities you look for in a performer who is auditioning?
'Personality' – you can't teach that – and a willingness to be open and explore. The excitement is the unknown. The process is my passion, not the end result. If we do our jobs right, the show will be there.

Do you believe that performers really can be a 'triple threat'?
Oh yes! They really need to be in this day and age. You must master your craft. It used to be that a triple threat actually excelled in one or two areas, but now I say you need to be a 'quad': a triple threat that does it all, and does it all brilliantly.

Which musical, in your experience, is the most challenging in terms of choreography?
West Side Story and shows like that are the most challenging because the dance is placed in the foreground as the prime indicator of story. Dance takes the role of dialogue. Shows like this require knowledge of mime, history, styles and story. A dance might look great, but in *WSS* you use the movement to express culture, emotion and plot. It's challenging and thrilling at the same time.

Which dance styles have most influenced shows you have worked on?
There are choreographers like Bob Fosse who had his own style. He used this style in all of his shows. Other choreographers use different styles of dance from the past and in some instances use multiple styles of dance that fit the culture of the show. Jack Cole used East Indian, Afro-Cuban and Lindy Hop in his work, and we call that 'jazz dance'; he called it street dance, dance of the people. I think Mr Cole, Mr Robbins and Mr Fosse, along with Mr Balanchine, have influenced me the most. Remember, before Robbins and Fosse there was Cole!

ANTHONY WHITEMAN, London: dancer, choreographer, teacher. Recent choreographic work includes *Legally Blonde, The Wizard of Oz, Bye Bye Birdie* and a new musical, *Dracula*.

What are the qualities you look for in a performer who is auditioning?
I am looking for technique, style and performance ability as well as trying to gauge the individual's work ethic and personality. Being relaxed and confident as well as having determination and eagerness for the project are essential qualities. Of course, key ingredients of every audition are the 'right look' and versatility.

What do you expect the cast to bring to their first rehearsal in terms of knowledge and understanding of the show?
An awareness of the musical and evidence that they have considered relevant background research so that they are self-informed about the work they are going to undertake. If it is a pre-existing show, they should take time to see it in performance. The cast need to be aware of the director's/choreographer's prior work and discover as much about the show as they can. When it is a new project, a lot of the research will be undertaken in rehearsal, but knowledge is power, so the cast should have some ideas about the work. I would expect them to engage with the libretto and pick up as many clues as possible from the audition process. Arriving in the rehearsal room with no knowledge isn't a great start to a happy contract.

Do you believe that a performer really can be a 'triple threat'?
I do believe that a performer can, and in this day, should really be a triple threat. I don't think it is necessary that all facets of dance/voice/drama are

equal, as everyone has various strengths and weaknesses, but they should be as skilled and rounded as possible. I know that I was capable as a performer in all three areas, although never the best in one aspect. I also feel that there is now a new fourth element: tumbling and acrobatics, which has been developing as an edge or trick to add to a performer's range.

How do you think that choreography contributes to the show(s) you are currently working on?

I have worked on shows where the choreography has been the driving force behind the production. Those I have choreographed have had a youthful energy: a huge factor that needs to be harnessed and moulded to help convey the story when there is no spoken or vocal text. In many cases the choreography doesn't just begin and end with the dance steps that the ensemble performs. There is the choreography of scene changes and musical staging which is usually undertaken by the choreographer. This often goes unnoticed but has been a major factor in every show in which I have been involved. I further believe that choreography helps actors to find and realise their character.

MICHAEL THOMAS VOSS, London: dancer, choreographer, teacher. Recent productions include *Princess Caraboo, Road Show, Saturday Night, Putnam 25th Annual Spelling Bee, Princess Ida* (nominated for Best Choreographer award), *Finian's Rainbow* and *A Little Night Music*.

What are the qualities you look for in a performer who is auditioning?

Personality, manners and first impressions! Performance qualities such as confidence, versatility and a good eye for detail are also helpful. Performers need to demonstrate their technical skills through their control, quality and musicality. They should bring something to the table that would enable them to make the character their own.

Do you believe that a performer really can be a 'triple threat'?

Yes, there is no reason why that shouldn't be possible, even if that means the three categories are placed at different levels. However, having said this, I come across too many actors who make excuses and try to wriggle themselves out of certain responsibilities rather than facing their weak points and working to fix them for future work. I believe that you can 'bring up' your weaker skill and even turn that into your strength. The whole idea and nature of musical theatre comedy is based around the drama, dance and song and the integration of these three disciplines. To be aware of all three disciplines makes for a stronger performer and seems to be working in America, so why not in the United Kingdom?

How do you think that choreography contributes to the show(s) you are currently working on?

Choreography in my current show is setting up action, time and location, and enabling the action to move swiftly from one scene to the next. This needs to happen with ease and to encompass the various demands of the libretto and score which require time lapses/flashbacks and memories and illustration of narration. Choreography can enhance everything from costume to storyline, period and emotion. It often functions as an important part of the show by commencing and concluding the narrative. It can identify the period, style and 'feel' of the musical; the movement can also bring attention to the movement qualities of the costumes, where appropriate. Choreography can set up, enliven a scene and/or make fun of a topic or set up and allow for super-imposed ideas. It can be used to create stylised storytelling and visualise a context or environment and to evoke emotions without using text. Choreography enables the audience to be taken to different places and have different thought processes: this gives the show depth and a variety of layers and dimensions.

Are dancing and singing in a musical a form of acting?

Definitely yes! Dancing enhances the character, whether in terms of looks and personality or by showing the actor in a certain emotional state, as well as progressing the plot or interjecting a thought/memory or context. The movement can enhance and emphasize the actor's lines or actions, act as an empowerment or even contradict in order to say something unexpected. You cannot separate the disciplines. As a performer, you need physicality, projection of energy, focus and intention the minute you step on stage. Even in stillness.

DAVID ASHLEY, London: professional dancer, director, teacher. West End performances include *Cats* and *Cabaret*.

What are the qualities you look for in a performer who is auditioning?

The main qualities I look for are discipline, artistry, dynamics through light and shade and, above all, enjoyment. Love of the material and the work is so very important.

What do you expect the cast to bring to their first rehearsal in terms of knowledge and understanding of the show?

I would expect a new company to have researched the world they will be exploring and gained a working knowledge of it as well as some knowledge of the piece – understanding of the narrative and overarching spine.

How do you think that choreography contributes to the show(s) you are currently working on?

It allows the narrative to develop and move forward. The choreography of Agnes de Mille in such musicals as *Oklahoma!* led the way in this work, and I believe from this development, the choreography of a production is an integral element to the overall storytelling.

Which musical, in your experience, is the most challenging in terms of choreography?

Cats, owing to the innovative and complex choreographic language Gillian Lynne created for it and the need to be totally immersed in that world as an actor.

GEORGE KIRKHAM, dance educator and Principal of Creative Academy, London. Recent productions include *Moulin Rouge*.

When auditioning what are the qualities you look for in a performer?

Passion, energy and physical technique.

Do you believe that a performer really can be a 'triple threat'?
To be a triple threat you must be an actor, dancer and singer. That level of training is highly specialised and available to the few: you cannot simultaneously reach the ability of world-class actors, singers and dancers. In a lifetime I think individuals can be an expert in one area and confident in the other two.

Which dance styles have most influenced shows you have worked on?
Jazz Technique, Commercial, Release and Graham.

How important is it to use the 'original choreography' for a show written in the past?
Not at all. The creation of new choreography brings excitement and updates the musical for a modern audience. Contemporary audiences are far more sophisticated with their access to the various media including TV, film and Internet. New choreography can reflect this, perhaps with a 'nod' to the past.

EMMA EVANS, British choreographer and dance educator.

Identify the title of the most recent musical(s) you have worked on.
BA Musical Theatre production, final-year students, London College of Music – *Alfie the Musical*.

What are the qualities you look for in a performer who is auditioning?
I don't expect a performer to be a proficient dancer, but to have a level of physical awareness.

What do you expect the cast to bring to their first rehearsal in terms of knowledge and understanding of the show?
Depending on the production, a level of social/historical knowledge.

Do you believe that a performer really can be a 'triple threat'?
I believe there are a few performers whom I can call a triple threat. You will find even the 'greats' are not as strong in one of the three disciplines.

How do you think that choreography contributes to the show(s) you are currently working on?
It contributes stylistically as well as helping to move the show's storyline/journey.

Are dancing and singing in a musical a form of acting? Undoubtedly, when you can no longer express yourself using the spoken word, the physical self and sung voice take over.

Which musical in your experience has been the most challenging in terms of choreography?
A youth theatre production of *West Side Story* in the round: certainly challenging, but highly rewarding in terms of seeing the actors, a number of whom were inexperienced in musical theatre, develop and grow as performers.

Which dance styles have most influenced shows you have worked on?
Fosse. Stylistically, his form of dance embodies my training and physicality.

How important is it to use the 'original choreography' for a show written in the past?

This depends upon the show. Certain choreography seems to be embedded in and synonymous with a musical: think of *West Side Story, Chicago* or *Cabaret*. Yet in the recent West End production of *Cabaret*, the choreography was completely reworked. *West Side Story* is another story: the original choreography has to be performed.

Self-reflection

Pause now before going on to read the final set of answers. Thinking about the various responses and comments provided by these practitioners and experts in the field of choreography, identify your personal understanding of what is required of you as a performer in musical theatre. Identify how you aim to achieve these in the time available to you in your studies, before considering this profession as a career choice.

When auditioning, what are the qualities you will wish to communicate to the audition panel?

How will you prepare for and hopefully secure success at your first audition?

Now read Barbara Hartwig's responses, and with all that you have read in mind, answer the questions we have posed you.

BARBARA HARTWIG: US choreographer

Identify the title of the most recent musical(s) you have worked on.
In October 2015, I choreographed *Mary Poppins* for the Gainesville Theatre Alliance in Gainesville, Georgia, just north of Atlanta. The Gainesville Theatre Alliance is a nationally acclaimed collaboration between the University of North Georgia, Brenau University, Theatre Professionals and the Northeast Georgia Community.

When auditioning what are the qualities you look for in a performer?
I look for someone who is prepared, professional, positive, quick to learn, takes direction well and, of course, has talent and stage presence.

What do you expect the cast to bring to their first rehearsal in terms of knowledge and understanding of the show?
The cast should have already read the script and have an understanding of their character and the characters they interact with. They should bring their own ideas to the table while being open to the director's vision. They should be prepared with the tools they need for rehearsal, such as scripts, pencils, recording devices for vocal parts, dance shoes, rehearsal wear and water.

Do you believe that a performer really can be a 'triple threat'?
Absolutely! There are amazingly talented people who are strong singers, dancers and actors. Usually one skill is their true strength and where they land most comfortably; however, the person is still a strong artist in the other two areas as well. Sometimes an artist is strong in four areas, if they play an instrument well. I saw a true example of a wonderful triple threat when I went to see *An American in Paris* on Broadway. The lead male was a beautiful ballet dancer with a lovely singing voice, and he lived honestly in the character. It was an all-round great performance.

How do you think that choreography contributes to the show(s) you are currently working on?
Dance is the extension of one's emotion. It is said that when you can no longer express your feelings through words (dialogue or lyrics), you dance. The choreography brings feelings and stories to life through movement. I feel even the simplest choreography can be extremely effective if it comes from the heart and motivation of the actors and is also an extension of the music. Musical numbers bring the energy of a show up and drive the story through song and dance. It must be a continuation of the story and be motivated by what happened just before the number began. Then the musical number needs to propel the scene that happens just after.

Are dancing and singing in a musical a form of acting?
When an actor can no longer express his or her feelings and emotions through dialogue, he or she sings and/or dances. It is an extension of the dialogue.

Music alone triggers an emotional response in its listeners, and when you add a story, words, movement and motivation behind that music, it can become extremely powerful and tell the story better than words or music alone. Isn't that the job of the actor – to tell a story and to get the audience to feel something? Actors can do that through singing and dancing as well.

Which musical in your experience is the most challenging in terms of choreography?
Wow! This is a difficult question, because the answer will be different with each choreographer, depending on what his or her strengths are. What may come easily for one may be very challenging for another. As far as what I consider to be the most challenging, it would have to be a show that stems from a very particular style of dance with which I am not very familiar. I would then need to do extensive research on the dance and its origin to successfully create the style and feel for the piece. A few examples of this would be *The Lion King* (African dance and animal movements), *Fiddler on the Roof* (Jewish heritage and traditional dances) or a show that takes place in a particular time period with which I am not familiar.

Which dance styles have most influenced shows you have worked on?
I come from a ballet background, so ballet has always been a strong influence for me when working on musicals. I admire the technical aspects and the beauty of the lines. I have created and put my style of dance on numerous musicals I have worked on, but I have also been asked to recreate the styles of great choreographers such as Bob Fosse, Jerome Robbins, Michael Bennett, Tommy Tune, Gillian Lynne and Susan Stroman. When choreographing, I am influenced by (i) all of my experiences as a performer and choreographer; (ii) my training and all of the styles I have learned from my wonderful teachers/choreographers over the years; (iii) all of the shows, dancers and dance performances that have inspired me over the years; (iv) the vision and inspiration of my director; (v) the strengths and talent of my performers. I then incorporate all of this together to create the best possible dance numbers and production.

Do you feel that the musical has become a global commodity? If so, what is the alternative?
I feel the modern-day musical is much more available to countries around the world than it used to be. However, there are many parts of the world in which this art form has never existed. I feel that the musical theatre community is definitely trying to reach a larger audience through the productions that have been aired on television recently, such as *The Sound of Music Live*, *Peter Pan Live*, *The Wiz Live* and *Grease Live*. Even though some of these musicals may not have been very successful, they reached an audience of people who might never have experienced a musical otherwise. People can also access many musicals and musical numbers on YouTube and other sites online. Some musicals are available on DVD and Netflix. This is great, but there really is really no comparison to seeing a musical performance in person. Musicals on Broadway have also changed a great deal in order to reach out to a different breed of audience. A huge example of this is the success of *Hamilton* (2015). I think tours used to

be more common in the United States and in Europe in the 1980s and 1990s. I don't believe there are as many productions or companies touring today. I also think it is very difficult to afford to see quality productions today. The prices of Broadway, West End and touring shows have skyrocketed to the point of no longer being accessible to many. People simply can't afford it.

How important is it to use the 'original choreography' for a show written in the past?

I think that depends on the vision of the director. There have been several occasions where I have been asked by the director to recreate the original choreography, and that is fine. I don't think it is necessary, however. Many times I believe that if a choreographer keeps the original integrity and style of the show, he or she can add their own flavour and self to it, and in doing so, create something unique and beautiful that still has the essence of the original. Sometimes, directors want to go into an entirely new direction, like bringing a period show to a modern-day setting. Therefore, the choreography would need to have more of a modern-day feel. I think it is all about what the director and choreographer envision and create as a team. As long as they work together and are on the same page, the choreography will be an extension of the scenes.

When you come to look back on your career, will you be able to draw on so wide a set of experiences as Barbara Hartwig? What can you learn from her extensive answers?

How will you cope with the demands of trying to be a 'triple threat' in order to increase your chances in audition and your opportunities for employment?

What personal strategies will you consider in aspects of your training if you are not successful at your first audition?

Discuss with your teachers and fellow students any areas of disagreement you may have noticed among the choreographers who answered our questions.

What answers would you have given to any of the questions posed: with whom did you agree or disagree most?

4 Critical Thinking in Musical Theatre

Using Part Four

Throughout this workbook you have considered the preparation of your body and voice to acquire skills and techniques associated with the art form of musical theatre and have been given opportunities to critically reflect on your learning. You have also been able to gain a personal philosophy and way of thinking to enable you to understand, manage and develop these ideas and techniques. By accessing these skills and repeating the technical tasks assigned, you have begun to enter the real world of performance.

However, your programme of work may well demand that you not only perform to the highest possible level but also submit term papers, essays, reviews and other forms of written evidence to show that you have understood the artistic and social implications of what you are doing and can demonstrate a range of critical skills. These include the ability to evaluate performances, place them in some historical context and form balanced judgements on what you see or participate in.

Very often, because their programme of study is largely practical, students become intimidated by the prospect of moving beyond the confines of a personal reflective journal to the more public and formal demands of academic writing. This fear is totally unnecessary because the very discipline in which students of musical theatre operate already provides a basis for their more formal analytical thinking and writing. The ability to express thoughts in writing is no more or less demanding than doing so through singing or dancing, and our particular aspect of performance is in constant need of those who can write perceptive and intelligent reviews or provide programme notes or project proposals that engage readers and enhance the value of a performance.

This section provides practical guidance for written work that is the result of good, clear, critical thinking, and we suggest that you begin by considering, perhaps in a way that you have never thought before, what is involved in 'rehearsal'. This may seem to be a strange way of cultivating critical thinking, but it is precisely that ability to analyse, evaluate, understand and discuss a process that may be very familiar that enables us to sharpen our critical faculties and consider the process as a phenomenon to be studied and appreciated. The very fact that you may have frequently engaged with an activity can often stand in the way of your being able to stand back from it and articulate its form and purpose. So approach the pages which follow with an open mind, as if you were thinking about the topic for the first time.

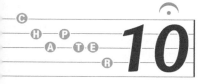

10 Critical Reflection and the Rehearsal Process

At some point in your studies there will be opportunities for the disciplines of acting, voice and dance to become integrated as elements of your performance work, and an ideal situation for such integration to be tested is the rehearsal process. Most rehearsals take place in appropriate spaces and provide a framework for structured thinking through performance workshops, experiment, new writing or devised work.

It is quite likely that the repetition of exercises associated with the rehearsal process has been a constant point of discussion among your peers as you have questioned their purpose and impact upon your own personal development. However, the word 'rehearsal' implies an important aspect of our craft – repetition. It is worth noting that the French word for rehearsal is *répétition* and the Italian, *ripetizione*. Obviously it is part of those cultures to associate repetition with progress towards the final performance.

By studying the various chapters in this book, you will now have realised that by

1. accepting the art of performance and being prepared to perform, *you have identified yourself as the central focus in this work.*
2. adopting the techniques given intellectually or physically, *you have shown yourself willing to complete the task.*
3. incorporating all your technical and creative skills and using them through an appropriate medium, you are communicating through musical theatre that *you are a performer.*
4. indulging in critical reflection on your personal development as a performer and understanding and articulating what you have achieved, *you have now entered the world of the scholar.*

As (i) a performer and (ii) a scholar, write a few sentences as to why repetition is such an important factor in the work of the performer. How do you feel when doing this work? Why might it have an impact upon the rehearsal process?

If you feel that repetitive work is boring, then you need to rethink your philosophy and try to understand why you have this attitude. Consider the words of a pre-Socratic philosopher, Heraclitus (c. 535–475 BC), who suggested that 'no one can step twice into the same river', thus encouraging us to think that doing something again will always be a different experience, although the action appears to be the same.

General rehearsal process

Remember that an important aspect of this work is how people are going to observe, trust, and think about *you*. As you enter the rehearsal room, you have everything going for you. You have worked hard at all the skills, and you are charming, willing to work and now in a position to put these into practice and contribute to the work of your peers in order create a memorable performance. What can go wrong?

Think about one particular rehearsal event in your recent studies, and comment on how you prepared for it. How did your peers react to you in this first rehearsal?

Having recalled that rehearsal, consider the following points:

1. What did you personally hope to achieve?
2. Can you comment upon your peers' expectations of you and of your work in the rehearsal?
3. What did you actually achieve in terms of the rehearsal expectations?

Whatever your responses, you can be assured that this is a thought process that many of us have been through in order to understand ourselves and, more importantly, the needs of others. Sometimes problems occur when you realise that other actors in the rehearsal room are not so well informed as you think you are, but still manage to do better than you do. Having both a high level of skill and thinking that you are on 'top of your game' is a tension that needs to be monitored carefully.

Follow-up work: Analyse an entire day in rehearsal with a fellow performer and see what transpires in conversation following the event. This will provide food for further thought.

Before we discuss general rehearsal issues, it is essential that we make sure that we know ourselves well enough to work in the rehearsal room at an optimum level of competence. Sometimes it is apparent that performers are not aware of why they have been chosen for a specific role in a play, musical or even an improvised scene. They are unaware of the personal qualities that they communicate to their peers.

Consider a play or musical you know well. Look into the mirror for a moment, and then answer the following important questions:

Which character do you feel you could portray with ease. Give reasons why.

Which character would you love to play if given the chance? What do you think might prevent this from happening?

Which character do you think the director would find you most suited to play? Why?

From all these observations is there anything that you might consider changing about yourself in order to achieve your potential performance goals? How are you going to achieve such a change?

Many of the issues we have discussed will relate to the general process of rehearsal enabling you to identify a range of strategies that you might consider using in order to get the best out of yourself and the company. In this way you can contribute to a positive atmosphere in the rehearsal room. Clearly, every performance piece has its own set of problems, and as a result no rehearsal process will be the same.

Identify two different rehearsal projects and specify a few similarities and differences.

Hopefully, from your notes and reflections you will have realised that your studies are in fact the most important aspect of your success in the rehearsal room. Never forget moments of uncertainty, and even failure, because they are major factors contributing to your eventual success. Gather the various experiences and formalise them into a personal paradigm that will enable you to see how vital your learning is to your achieving your goals.

Specify a time frame and then consider the following ideas and make comments:

Time frame	
From:	**To**
What did you want to achieve?	Did you achieve it?
Whom did you work with?	Has this changed, and if so, why?
Identify moments of success:	How did this help you progress?
What did you know?	What do you know now?

The First Stage of the Rehearsal

Although for many reasons no two rehearsal processes will be the same, there are certain factors that will remain constant following the initial casting process.

The first stage of a rehearsal is the discussion centring on how the production is to proceed. This is an opportunity for all the company to be involved and to make their mark on the rehearsal process. In the best possible scenario, one can hope to engage with the following:

1. Scenic design with a model or at least sketches of how the set will work and influence the production.
2. Elements of the scoring or underscoring to assist with certain moods and properties within the production.
3. Additional stimuli such as magazines, journals, paintings, DVDs, CDs, poetry, images and additional artefacts that encourage a useful discussion about the content, structure, style and mood of the production.
4. Creative staff involved with the production.

Note to yourself: You can see already how many people are involved in the production process, so be aware of how you come to that first meeting. Be mentally prepared and focused. Consult your notes. Did you consider meeting with the various departments involved with the production in your individual preparation notes?

Often this is the stage of rehearsal when most discussion takes place. Some directors discuss everything with their actors before a single move is plotted (intellectual response), and others get the actors on their feet from the very start (kinaesthetic response).

Which style of rehearsal would you prefer? Why? Analyse what these ideas say about you as a performer. What might you consider in the future?

Other rehearsal devices include ensemble exercises, improvisation work, creative warm-ups and theatre games that relate to the production being prepared.

Discuss your ideal rehearsal process and why it suits you personally.

As musicals have a score as well as a libretto (dialogue), all performers are required to learn 'the dots' before the main work can commence. It is also at this first stage of the rehearsal process that we can instigate discussions about the work. The most important factor here is to create a positive thinking ground devoid of negativity or bad moods. All too frequently discussions in student productions get bogged down with politics and personalities. Everyone wants to be heard. Remember that the essential qualities in a performer are the ability to recognise who he or she is and to make decisions that reflect a positive state of mind.

Make it your challenge to find out about different approaches to the rehearsal process. Research the work of various famous directors to find out as much as you can about their different or similar ways of rehearsing. Some of the most rewarding directors to investigate are listed here:

Konstantin Stanislavski

Peter Brook

Deborah Warner

Tyrone Guthrie

Susan Stroman

Hal Prince

Nicholas Hytner

Edward Gordon Craig

Katie Mitchell

If, for example, you research the work of Peter Brook, you will encounter his book *The Empty Space* (1968), which will provide you with profound insights into theatre and its processes. Furthermore, *The Making of A Midsummer Night's Dream* (1982), by David Selbourne, provides an excellent account of the rehearsal processes employed by Brook and will give you a great deal to reflect upon as you follow your performing career.

Find out as much as you can about any director you encounter as part of your studies, and identify his or her individual approaches to the rehearsal room and the entire production process. This will prepare you for your first professional rehearsal and give you some indications of what to expect when cast in your first professional role.

The Second Stage of Rehearsal

Getting the production on its feet...

The rehearsal space is preferably similar to the final performance space in terms of its dimensions. The stage manager will have set the stage boundaries with a mark-up, and most objects (props) will have been acquired so that the performers can get used to all the physical aspects of the delivery of their role. There may be times when this is not possible, but these are few and far between, and the designer will be a constant companion to the director in order that the design remains appropriate to the decisions made.

Often the production is approached through the narrative so that the cast are made aware of the consequences of actions taken by each character. However, there may be many variations on this approach. For example, there was an occasion when a director who was working on Stephen Sondheim's *Merrily We Roll Along* decided to rehearse each scene in reverse order: beginning from the end of the musical.

Investigate the musical *Merrily We Roll Along*, and find out why this might have happened. Can you think of other musicals with interesting structures that might require different rehearsal approaches, for example *The Last Five Years* by Jason Robert Brown?

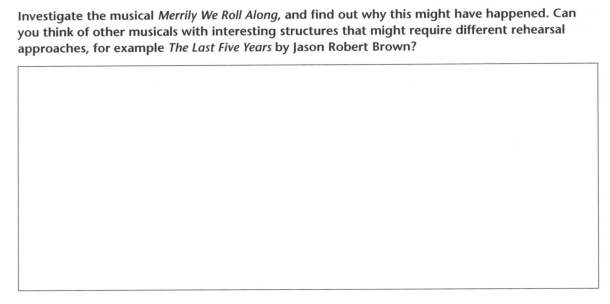

This second stage of the rehearsal is often referred to as 'blocking'. This involves the choreographer and musical director, and more often than not the larger music and dance numbers are rehearsed in one room while the director works with some smaller ensemble moments in another – if space allows.

There are many ways of thinking about the purpose of this stage in the rehearsal process, and it often depends on the narrative content and form of the musical production. Sometimes the action needs to be taken out of sequence in order for the performers to fully understand their position within the play. However, decisions about the rehearsal sequence are always in the hands of the director, and so you should be prepared for any eventuality. Some like to look at the entire musical production and add no detail, whereas others work in detail before moving on to the next scene. There is definitely no wrong or right way to proceed. Take care not to comment upon this directorial process in the rehearsal room. Any dissent will have negative consequences.

You need to understand how the director works as soon as possible because there are expectations in terms of your dealing with the rehearsal process. Some directors expect you to remember exactly what they did yesterday and are very prescriptive in their behaviour, whereas others are happy for the performers to 'find their own way', and so experiment until an agreed version has been achieved in an organic fashion. You will find some methods illuminating and stimulating, and others will challenge your reason and patience. Your job as a performer is to rehearse, not judge the method by which the production eventually comes to fruition. Once the project is complete, you will be in a position to evaluate and analyse what has taken place. One thing is certain: you are the performer for a reason, and you have been chosen for your skill. It is expected that you will bring imagination, creativity and a willingness to behave in a spontaneous manner so that the director can use your skills as an inspirational tool.

Think about the last production you were involved in: what methods did the director use to achieve the final performance? Analyse the actual process in relation to the form and structure of the production.

Some directors hold company discussions at points during the rehearsal process in order that the actions are reviewed and questions are asked to resolve any uncertainties about interpretation. This is a stimulating way to work, but do not be disappointed if the rehearsal room is not a place for democracy.

The final part of this stage is setting the ideas and realising that specific movements and actions must be associated with particular lines, entrances and exits. There are many ways of dealing with this work, and many different demands will be made of you.

Some directors will insist that you are 'off book' at the start of the rehearsal process, whereas other directors may not want you to learn the lines until much later. This should not be a problem – the easiest solution is to be 'off book' always and then act by reading the words if required by the director.

Identify moments in a rehearsal when being 'off book' was essential.

The Third Stage of Rehearsal

From the investigation of the creative detail to the 'sitzprobe' and the final 'dry-run'

This stage is the creative moment when the broad paint strokes of the blocking process have been placed on the canvas, and the focus is now on details that will bring shapes and colours to the imaginary world of the production. It is the opportunity for the text, choreography and music to be understood and explored in minute detail. This is the time to listen carefully to each word spoken or sung and to observe the clarity of each movement and realise the nuance of each expression. This is often the most exciting part of the production and yet is sometimes never reached because of bad planning or inadequate rehearsal time.

There are opportunities at this stage of the production work for a director to *either* run through without stopping *or* 'stagger' through sections of the musical, looking at each moment in detail in conjunction with the musical director and choreographer, dissecting every aspect of the production.

This is often the stage when feedback (detailed notes) is given by the key members of the production team so that the performers can understand what they have to do for the next rehearsal. These situations can be very difficult to manage, and frequently time is the deciding factor. For example, the time when notes are most needed may be at the end of the day, but because the cast are exhausted or anxious to go home, this can be a very bad time to give them. However, commencing the next day with critical notes might mean a negative start with little time to absorb their content. What would you do?

If you were a director, how would you deal with feedback to your cast? Consider the overall rehearsal process, and give some analytical insight into your reasons. Talk to your next director about this if you get an opportunity.

There is one further stage before going into the main performance space where the production is to take place: the *sitzprobe* ('sit and explore'). This is the time when company and musicians meet for the first time under the baton of the musical director. The intention here is to sing through every note and interrogate every aspect of the score, including underscoring (music to create a specific moment and heartbeat within the action) where relevant. This process is sometimes a little daunting as you may well be asked to sing against an orchestra or band without microphones because sound equipment is not available at this stage. Be prepared for this, and don't be disappointed if you can't always hear yourself – you will.

As musicals are such giants of production management, the sound, lighting and costumes will often only come together throughout the final week of rehearsals. The opportunity will therefore be taken to do a 'dry run' to enable lighting and sound technicians to register specific details and the costume department to note quick changes and any other fine details.

There will usually be one run through to provide all the creatives with an opportunity to have a final look at the work: this may be when invited personnel from the production company might attend to see the end product before it moves into the theatre. Again, be prepared for this: it is no longer the time for the cast to be rehearsing; it is now the time to perform.

The Fourth Stage of Rehearsal

Technical to final dress rehearsal in the actual performance space
Lights, set, sound and costume come together in a blaze of glory, high energy and sometimes confusion. This is the culmination of what everyone has been working for – when the fruits of all the visionary work are put to the test. You will meet all those creatives again, but now you will see them in a different light. They have fulfilled their tasks and are now expecting you to make good all your promises. The most frustrating thing for the cast is that you are no longer the star performers of the show. You simply need to speak cues and move with accuracy so that sound and lighting cues can be set.

There are two phases you can expect in these rehearsals. The first might appear obvious as it looks at each cue in turn and checks that all is well. The second is to run a section of the production non-stop and then reflect on the success of that 'run' before moving on to the next section of the production. This is known as a 'dry teching' and will involve lights and costume. The climax of this work is in the formal technical rehearsal before the dress rehearsal. You must realise that the director is no longer in control of running the show as he or she hands over to the creatives and the stage manager. The director now sits in the auditorium, takes notes for the dress rehearsal and communicates with all creatives and cast after that and during the run of the show.

Identify your own experiences in a musical production by discussing the rehearsal process, audience response, recorded materials and personal memories. Compare and contrast your ideas with those detailed in this chapter. What are the main differences?

The Final Stage

The fall of the curtain

The performance has ended, and each member of the production team – company and creatives – return to their specific place of work to consider the event. Hopefully they are able to reflect on a wonderful experience enjoyed by audience and production team alike. Following all the excitement of the performance, you are now required to move from the imaginary world back to the world of reality. How do we learn how to cope with such sharp transitional changes in our lives? We have concentrated so much on the 'doing' and 'performing' that we often forget the normality of life.

In your experience as a performer, what have you noted about the moments or periods of inactivity after a performance. Can you track a series of events that have taken place? If so, analyse them to see what you understand about this period of time.

Clearly this is an important aspect of our existence. Some performances can live on well beyond the lives of those involved in the actual event. But most will reappear in journals, reviews and a variety of other recorded materials that serve to preserve the memory. We might think of Peter Brook's memorable production of *A Midsummer Night's Dream* that we cited earlier. (see p.120) The impact of this example of Brook's directorial work continues and has remained famous or regarded as seminal over decades – well after the 'first night party'. Can you explain why this should be? Musical theatre productions that have lived on in the memory would include *Sweeney Todd*, directed by Hal Prince; *West Side Story*, directed by Jerome Robbins; *Oklahoma!*, directed by Rouben Mamoulian (more famous for its choreographer Agnes de Mille); and *Cabaret*, directed by Hal Prince. What were the qualities of these productions that ensured their long afterlife?

Through the process of creation, rehearsal and performance, we are now also involved both with memory and critical evaluation as a means of understanding what has taken place. So the cycle is complete when our research enables us to investigate what has gone before and to appreciate the choices which must be made in order to communicate with an audience.

It is therefore fitting that as the final task for this chapter you undertake some research that engages with these ideas and encourages you to interrogate this world of musical theatre with which you have become so familiar. Look with new eyes and a deeper sense of truth. You will be amazed by what you will discover about yourself, your art and the world around you.

FINAL TASK
A research project

Investigate a popular performance of historical note through materials, journals, newspaper columns, DVDs, CDs and any other relevant materials. By this research alone, aim to suggest whether in today's society this performance would have had the same impact upon an audience. What does this suggest about performance and society?

How do these performances live on? Is it important, or is it an aspect of the world of performance that we haven't yet embraced?

Writing a Theatre Review

At some stage in your career in musical theatre, you will either be required to write a theatre review as an essay, term paper, article or journal entry *or* you will anxiously await the review of a production in which you have been involved. To benefit from any of these situations, it is necessary to understand the nature of a good review and appreciate the role of theatre criticism in your life.

You may well have come to this topic with previously formed views, but, as with every area of study approached in this book, we would ask you to consider some fundamental questions with fresh thinking. In the boxes provided respond to these questions, and then compare your answers with our discussion on the pages following:

What is a theatre review?

What is a theatre critic?

What qualifies you to become a critic of musical theatre?

Discussion

1. An acceptable theatre review is an unbiased and informed critical account of a performance. It contains elements of information and of critical analysis. It provides a permanent record of a production, and before the invention of various mechanical forms of recording, it may have been the only means of preserving the ephemeral nature of theatre. A review is *not* about finding fault or heaping praise: it may well need to have aspects of this kind of response, but its main purpose is to inform potential audiences of what they might expect to experience in general terms and to evaluate the quality of the work presented.

   Reviews are sometimes responsible for the failure of a production to achieve a substantial run or, conversely, for the unexpected success of some previously unknown performer or new work. A good, constructive review assists directors, choreographers, musicians and other artists to think critically about their own contribution and to understand what an audience might 'read' from what they see and hear. Ideally, a review enables the participants to benefit from outside judgements that are based on an awareness of universal standards.

   There have been examples of where a single review has changed the critical reaction to a piece that has been previously given a very negative reception.

2. A theatre critic is not someone whose job it is to find fault. There are many forms of criticism in the arts, but none of them should rely on the critic

coming to the work with a preconceived idea and then judging what they see, read or hear by those fixed principles. A good theatre critic writes interestingly about the arts and brings a breadth of theatre performance experience so that he or she is able to make valid appraisals and comparisons. Sometimes a critic wishes to champion the work of a particular artist, creator or group because the critic feels that it deserves wider notice and appreciation. The best critics convey a sense of the experience of being present at a performance and support all their arguments and points with clear examples and evidence. Some critics may come to a production with profound knowledge of the work being performed, but others might freely admit to having no prior knowledge of the work and evaluate the experience of being introduced to the work through performance. A good critic does not waste time and space by trying to demonstrate how much he or she knows about the work being presented.

3. There have been many examples in the past of critics who have a very limited experience of theatre and have only acquired an ability to write well by frequent visits to performances. This is not an ideal situation, and not one we would recommend. It is far better to approach the task of reviewing with a body of knowledge and preferably with some experience of performance. Far more important for musical theatre, however, is an understanding of the genre itself and a realisation that a successful and meaningful performance can only be achieved through the integration of the various theatre arts. In musical theatre, elements of poetry, spoken text, acting, dancing, design and music (both vocal and instrumental) combine to create a new art form, and a critic must notice all these elements. On the other hand, a critic must also recognise that theatre is a mode of storytelling that can be profoundly moving, amusing, life affirming or tragic. This is just as true of musical theatre as it is of any other form of theatre, and unless the narrative element of a production is clear and powerful, the audience, of which a critic is the representative, will be frustrated and entitled to express negative opinions. To be an effective critic of musical theatre, you must be able to comment on all aspects of a production, and every experience you have during your programme of study will enable you to undertake the role of critic more successfully. This, of course, is only true if you constantly reflect upon and analyse your experience.

When you have compared these statements with those you made in response to our questions, discuss them with your fellow students or teachers, and then think about the following two questions:

Is a critical study of performance useful to me?

Yes, the theories associated with the interdisciplinary field of performance underpin the disciplines of performance studies and communication studies, both of which have become popular during the last thirty years or so. Both of these disciplines have sometimes been seen to be at odds with the more practical theatre studies, and it is true that neither necessarily requires students to do any performing or communicating, but rather to discuss the processes involved. However, this is a narrow view, and rather like the necessary links between dancing and music in musical theatre, there are obvious points of common interest in all these disciplines. There are two particularly helpful concepts that a student and potential critic of musical theatre can draw from the more theoretically based subjects: the idea of 'reading' a performance and the hierarchy of art forms. Employing the terms used in communication studies, everything that is designed to communicate something is a 'text'. This may be visual, auditory, moving or static. Words are 'text' and so is a scenic design or a lighting change. A costume is a 'text' and so are dance steps or gestures. The point about a text is that we must 'read' it, and it is the ability to read a performance that a critic must develop. A critic must constantly ask, 'What is this telling me?' and apply the question to all aspects of a performance.

In performance studies there is no sense in which one kind of performance is 'greater' or more significant than another. Classical music is no greater and more worthy of serious attention than jazz, rock, folk or any form of popular music; the plays of Shakespeare are of no more value than improvised theatre; opera is not superior to the musical; hip-hop is not inferior to *Swan Lake*. This demolition of the traditional hierarchy in attitudes has benefited musical theatre, and the musical has become an item for serious appreciation and debate.

What do I look for and include when I write a review?

When you attend a performance or watch it via recorded media, it is useful to have a checklist of features to notice in preparation for your review: use the list below until you have gained sufficient experience to add more points of your own:

The event

1. Where and when did it take place?
2. What company was presenting the show?
3. How did you get to hear about it?
4. Was it part of a festival or similar event?
5. Was there anything particularly interesting or unusual about the venue?
6. Who were the director, musical director, designer and choreographer?

The work

1. What was the precise title of the work being presented?
2. Who were the writers/composers?
3. Was this a new work, or if not, when was it written?
4. What was the subject/topic/story of the work?
5. What particular demands did this work make?
6. Did it have a distinctive musical style, and if so, what?
7. When and where was the show set?
8. Did the show have new choreography or was the 'original' used?
9. Does this work have an afterlife?

The stage

1. What precise form of stage did the venue have, and how was it shaped?
2. What varieties of audience view/experience did this theatre/venue provide?
3. What were the stage settings, and how was lighting used to complement or contribute to these?
4. How did the cast use the stage?
5. Where was the band or group of musicians, or did the production rely on other forms of accompaniment?
6. How was the sound quality, and what means of amplification (if any) were used?

The production

1. Did the performances strike you as 'truthful' or 'natural'?
2. Was the storyline clear?
3. Were the various art forms well integrated, or was it obvious, for example, when a performer moved from 'acting' to singing?
4. What qualities of dance and song were obvious, and were you comfortable with them?
5. What did the costumes and décor contribute to the production?
6. Was everyone on stage 'in the moment' all the time, or were there lapses of concentration or involvement
7. Was the chorus (if there was one) a genuine 'character'?
8. Was the production of an acceptable length, or did it go on for too long?
9. Were there any outstanding performances on which you felt anxious to comment?

Writing your review

Be sure to ascertain the word length of your intended piece: requirements may vary considerably. Make a habit of reading theatre reviews in the press and online: wherever possible read at least two reviews of the same production. Once you have made your notes using our suggested checklist, remember that it is your job to convey a sense of the entire experience of attending the performance. Even though you may consider each element of the performance in turn, it is the synthesis of those elements that constitutes a performance event, so try not to become obsessed by one element that may have impressed or annoyed you. Theatre publicity often makes use of small quotations from reviews in order to attract customers: that is, of course, entirely legitimate, but try not to write a sequence of such statements in the hope of writing a striking piece. By all means express your enthusiasm, admiration or reservations, but do not become seduced by the language of advertising. For example, comment on the following statement used on the publicity for a recent production:

An excellent company of young performers: their energy and enthusiasm is breathtaking.

Our comment

Hopefully you have spotted the grammatical error: energy and enthusiasm are two separate qualities so it should read 'are breathtaking'. Errors such as this and the incorrect use of apostrophes are all too frequent on public documents. However, what does this statement about a company actually tell us? If they are young, how young are they? Why are they 'excellent' – is it just their energy and enthusiasm? If these qualities are worth commenting on, you will recall that we have suggested that 'energy' is a basic requirement of musical theatre, and so, of course, is enthusiasm. Why should these qualities take away anyone's breath when they are simply aspects of minimum competence? You need to be wary of statements that actually tell us virtually nothing about a performance.

Fortunately, a review need never be very long, and this should provide you with plenty of time to read it through. You have probably experienced a situation when a computer or similar electronic device refuses to work and you have been advised to 'switch it off' and then restart it some time later. That is good advice for a writer too. Always leave some time between your initial writing and making your revisions. A few hours' or, ideally, days' break will often achieve remarkable new perceptions and avoid unnecessary errors.

We wish you well in your endeavours.

Bibliography

Bartal, L., Ne Nira and N. Ne'eman (2002) *Movement, Awareness and Creativity* (United Kingdom: Dance Books).

Da Vinci, L. (2005) *The Notebooks* (London: Profile Books).

Ganzl, K. (1994) *Encyclopedia of the Musical Theatre* (New York: Schirmer).

Giddings, G. (2001) *Bing Crosby: A Pocketful of Dreams; the Early Years 1903–1940* (Boston: Little, Brown and Co).

Hare, D. (2015) *The Blue Touch Paper – A Memoir* (London: Faber and Faber).

Harwood, R. (1984) *All the World's a Stage* (London: Methuen).

Kenrick, J. (2010) *Musical Theatre: A History* (New York: Continuum).

Loveless, A. (2015) *Tess of the d'Urbervilles: A Musical* (London and New York: Samuel French).

Mettler, B. (2011) *The Nature of Dance as a Creative Art* Activity, available at https://www.hampshire.edu/sites/default/files/archives/mettler/NatureOfDance.pdf (accessed 23 May 2016).

Sunderland, M. and K. Pickering (2008) *Choreographing the Stage Musical* (California: Players Press).

Wigman, M., W. Sorell and C. Rudolph (1975) *The Language of Dance* (Middletown, CT: Wesleyan University Press).

Further Reading

Everett, W. and P. Laird (eds) (2008) *The Cambridge Companion to the Musical* (Cambridge: Cambridge University Press).

Gardyne, J. (2004) *Producing Musicals: A Practical Guide* (London: Crowood Press).

Guernsey, O. (ed.) (1964) *Playwrights, Lyricists, Composers on Theater* (New York: Dodd, Mead & Co).

Harvard, P. (2013) *Acting through Song* (London: Nick Hern Books).

Henshall, R. (2010) *So You Want to Be in Musicals* (London: Nick Hern Books).

Henson, D. and K. Pickering (2013) *Musical Theatre: A Workbook* (Basingstoke: Palgrave).

Jasper, T. and K. Pickering (2010) *Jesus Centre Stage* (Godalming: Highland).

Koner, P. (1993) *Elements of Performance: A Guide for Performers in Dance, Theatre and Opera* (Chur, Switzerland: Harwood Academic Publishers).

Mackintosh, C. (2010) *The Faber Pocket Guide to Musicals* (London: Faber and Faber).

Pickering, K. (2010) *Key Concepts in Drama and Performance* (Basingstoke: Palgrave Macmillan).

Porter, S. (1997) *The American Musical Theatre* (California: Players Press).

Sondheim, S. (2010) *Finishing the Hat* (London: Virgin Books).

Taylor, M. and D. Symonds (2014) *Gestures of Music Theatre* (New York: OUP).

Taylor, M. and D. Symonds (2014) *Studying Musical Theatre* (London: Palgrave).

Tebbutt, G. (2003) *Musical Theatre* (London: Dramatic Lines).

Wheeler, J. and H. Laughlin (1997) *Assignments in Musical Theatre* (California: Players Press).

Woolford, J. (2013) *How Musicals Work* (London: Nick Hern Books).

Index of Topics